What people ar

The Joy of Caring

Caring is all about presence. In being present, we care for someone's well-being. This joyful book presents the human art of caring as a future forming gesture ("presencing") inviting humanity to include, emerge and transcend. To read is to become embraced by Miriam's caring presence. Her book is a genuine present, once carefully unwrapped, offering the joy of a loving life.

Cees Hoogendijk, co-creator of Genarrativity

Such a generous and inspiring book – full of clear questions to ask ourselves and exercises to help us feel that joy of caring. Surprisingly perhaps, we're encouraged to start by being self-centred – by knowing ourselves better we can be better at being there for others.

There are dangers in caring and trying to help. As Miriam Subirana points out, too often we think we're helping by sharing our own problems or difficulties. Not only is this not helpful but we set up a dynamic that gets in the way. It is only when we take care of ourselves first that we can truly listen to the other. Then from this beautiful space between us the unexpected emerges and transforms the difficulties.

Miriam Subirana blends her extensive knowledge of different religions, practices and meditation approaches to provide not only the background for the seven sections but also the important questions to help us select the right steps. Living differently brings its paradoxes: doing less to achieve more; doing one task at a time instead of multitasking; and learning new habits to have less rather than more pressure in our lives.

The phrases and approaches with special resonance for me are about trusting in the power of letting go, being aware that much gratitude is already present, and being in my vital core is the place of full potential. Then the creativity and joy of transformation can flow.

Anne Radford, Appreciative Inquiry consultant and founder of Appreciative Inquiry Practitioner journal

The Joy of Caring

Transforming difficulties into possibilities

The Joy of Caring

Transforming difficulties into possibilities

Miriam Subirana

Translated by: Caroline Wilson

Original title: El placer de cuidarnos: Transforma las
dificultades en posibilidades

BOOKS

Winchester, UK
Washington, USA

JOHN HUNT PUBLISHING

First published by O-Books, 2021
O-Books is an imprint of John Hunt Publishing Ltd., 3 East St., Alresford,
Hampshire SO24 9EE, UK
office@jhpbooks.com
www.johnhuntpublishing.com
www.o-books.com

For distributor details and how to order please visit the 'Ordering' section on our website.

Text copyright: Miriam Subirana 2019

ISBN: 978 1 78904 492 8
978 1 78904 493 5 (ebook)
Library of Congress Control Number: 2019956111

A CIP catalogue record for this book is available from the British Library.

Design: Stuart Davies

UK: Printed and bound by CPI Group (UK) Ltd, Croydon, CR0 4YY
US: Printed and bound by Thomson-Shore, 7300 West Joy Road, Dexter, MI 48130

We operate a distinctive and ethical publishing philosophy in
all areas of our business, from our global network of authors to
production and worldwide distribution.

Contents

Introduction   1

1. Caring for Yourself   4
Self-image   7
Discovering and realising your full potential   12
Taking care of the self   16
The self and the soul   20
The value of the self   23

2. Being in Oneself   27
Being yourself   28
Being in your body   36
Being in your mind   40
Being in your heart   47
The vital core   54

3. Opening   58
Trust   62
Allowing yourself to be more creative   69
Letting go   72
Opening to feeling   75
Remembering and recycling   76
Gratitude   80
Relaxing and opening channels   81

4. Being in Relationship   83

5. Taking Care of Ourselves   89
Transforming difficulties into possibilities   89
Being present   112

Giving and giving from the self   119
Accepting   129
Welcoming   138

6. Taking Care of the Whole   **141**
Make peace with time: do less and achieve more   141
The joy of working   146
Spaces to care for oneself and be creative   151
Being in the world   152
What steps can we take to look after our world?
    Some questions, some facts...   158

7. Compassion and Contemplation   **162**
Compassion   162
Contemplation   168

Notes   **172**

Other O-Books by this author

Dare to Live (2008) 978 1 84694 120 7
Who Rules In Your Life? (2008) 978 1 84694 117 7
Live in Freedom (2009) 978 1 84694 196 2
Creativity to Reinvent Your Life (2010) 978 1 84694 361 4
From Neediness to Fulfillment (2013) 978 1 78099 129 0
Flourishing Together (2016) 978 1 78535 376 5

Are we able to find a way towards love and joy
at all times?

Introduction

We are living through a period characterised by a surge in individualism, the care of the body and of oneself. It is fashionable to go to the gym and the spa, to have massages and go running. We undertake all kinds of therapies, pay close attention to the food we eat and take vitamin supplements. There are numerous courses on offer to further self-knowledge and self-care. We are immersed in a culture that pushes us to improve ourselves, to cultivate our self-esteem and develop as people.

Of course, it's great that we are taking care of ourselves, and that we do so in the most respectful way, in harmony with the environment. Fantastic – as long as we don't get too self-obsessed and forget to look after our fellow human beings. This can and does happen, given that our culture cultivates the I, the me and mine. We look out too much for ourselves and what we want, which doesn't always coincide with what we need. If we fail to find a balance between self-care and caring for others, selfishness and egocentricity grow. Consumed with satisfying our nonessential desires and needs, we have created worldwide disharmony. Greed is the great enemy of both our own health and that of our planet.

When someone develops a habit of looking after themselves and what they consider to be theirs, they can become blind and deaf to the needs of others. They might even feel that taking care of others is a burden. If they do take on a caring role, it is often out of responsibility or obligation, not the joy of giving to the other and sharing from the self. Relationships turn into an encumbrance to such a degree that in the West many people live alone. How do we stop feeling that caring is nothing more than a duty or a burden?

I ask myself how we can go from the *I* to the *we* and from the *we* to the *I* with joy and fluidity, so that our relationships can flow between the *I*, the *you* and the *we*; how can we take off our masks and the defensive attitudes that divide and exhaust us? We will explore this in the pages to come.

Caring is so much more than just paying attention when there is sickness and pain. Caring is loving, appreciating, accepting, receiving, embracing, feeling and understanding. It is sharing, accompanying, healing, giving relief, inspiration and encouragement. It is co-creating. To care is to listen, to be present, available, open and attentive. **To care is to give oneself out of joy.** In this book I want to explore how you can take care of others and yourself without being overwhelmed and martyred by it; how you can look after yourself without blaming others or feeling guilty. I want to share with you how to look after yourself while also caring for relationships and the relational being.

Is it possible to connect to and take care of the other from a place of the joy of being, keeping our minds and hearts open and generous? How can we establish healthy relationships where we also take care of ourselves, so that we don't enter into saviour-victim or protector-protected dynamics? "How do we fight against a selfishness that has taken on huge proportions in our societies and generate a culture of compassion that we can have faith in?"[1]

What is the call, coming from within, urging us to care for and help others? What are the essential elements involved in looking after and supporting each other? When someone feels pain, when they are suffering, what really helps? What can we do that is genuinely beneficial? When should we give advice; when is our presence alone enough to show we care?

What are our intentions when we take care of someone? Why do we look after them? Do we really love them, accepting their ideas, feelings and way of being or, in truth, do we want to use them for our own ends? Do you sometimes want to help someone else so that you can feel good about yourself? Are you a saviour, the one who "has to" look after someone, or are you the friend who listens and accompanies? Or do you want the other person to change?

What did someone who looked after you well do or say? What have others done to offer you care that was useful and beneficial? In what way did they do it?

How can we understand ourselves at the same time as helping those around us?

What gets in the way of knowing how to really look after ourselves and each other, how to accompany and help one another?

"... what are the characteristics of those relationships that *do* help, which do facilitate growth? And at the other end of the scale, is it possible to discern those characteristics which make a relationship unhelpful, even though it was the sincere intent to promote growth and development?"[2]

These are some of the many questions that I ask and explore in the following pages.

Caring for ourselves is essential if we are to live with dignity and reach wholeness, to stop being hard on ourselves and let go of hopeless and useless inner dialogues. This book seeks to be an aid to learning how to really take care of ourselves; how to look after and accompany both ourselves and others in developing as creative, autonomous and emotionally mature people. To become strong and face life in a way that is more constructive, intelligent and sociable, and more satisfying as well.

1. Caring for Yourself

Real self-love cannot be distinguished from love of another.[3]
Peter Schellenbaum

To care for yourself you have to love yourself. You can only really take care of yourself if you are grounded in self-love. Otherwise, you are likely to be too hard on yourself. It's easy to say and write, but it's not so easy to put into practice. I hope this book helps make it easier.

There are three main factors that can sabotage our intentions to look after ourselves. These are: wanting to please others, feeling overly autonomous and independent, and caring too much about the opinions of others.

The ideal thing is to care out of love, freedom and respect. However, through attachment and fear, we might try to take care of ourselves in a way that can become suffocating. We do it out of obligation, because we believe there is no other option; we take care of ourselves because we are afraid that if we don't, something might go wrong.

For example, I think that doing exercise because you feel you have to is being too harsh with yourself. You don't enjoy the moment. You count the minutes, pressured by the desire to get results. Of course, it's important that looking after ourselves should bring good results, but when we feel under pressure to achieve specific goals, there is less love, tenderness and enjoyment of the moment in our self-care. It becomes one more obligation on our to-do list. This kind of care doesn't lead to a meaningful encounter with yourself; it is limited to merely carrying out activities that are good for the body.

Taking care of someone else can also be seen as another obligation on our to-do list, meaning we risk exhaustion through looking after them but not ourselves. If you don't want to get burnt out or lose touch with yourself, you have to understand how to look after yourself. "Caring for oneself is the condition that makes it possible to care for others in the right way."[4] To connect properly to the other, you need to know how to tune in to yourself and not stray from the path that keeps you in touch with your centre. It is not selfish to love yourself, to stay close to yourself and see and accept yourself. Only by doing so will you be able to take really good care of others.

In this book I want to share some experiences that have helped me to take care of my being. They have shown me how to live better and stop blaming myself or being a martyr. They have taught me not to turn desires into demands or dreams into unachievable expectations. I will also share the experiences of others I have accompanied for over thirty years, years devoted to contributing to people's creative, emotional, relational, spiritual and professional development. The examples help us to see reflections of experiences that might occur to us, as well as giving us guidelines that can be applied to our own lives.

Peter stopped dreaming because, in the past, his dreams had ended up in frustration. He decided to live in the present and not allow himself to dream. Little by little, his creative voice was stifled; there was no space left in his life for aspirations. When he took part in an Appreciative Inquiry training session, he realised the importance of recovering his dreams and aspiring to fulfil them. He was receptive again to his immense inner creative potential.

Hannah felt guilty whenever she spent time looking after herself, as if her life, which was spent giving to others, made her feel it was wrong to have time for herself. Bit by bit, she dried up inside and realised that she had stopped seeing herself; she had given up on herself. She did some inner work that opened her to look within and take care of herself. She dedicated a sacred and creative empty space to herself, allowing her to find vitality and happiness again and stop feeling guilty.

Martha had fallen in love with a man who didn't really want to share his life with her: he didn't want to be seen with her in public, only privately and at limited times. She was clear that she should stop thinking about him, that a relationship with no reciprocity or commitment on his part didn't suit her. However, she clung to the past, to what had been and, she believed, could be again, constantly beating herself up mentally with thoughts such as: "What if he does change in the end? It can't be that it seemed so good and then ended up like this so quickly. If I leave him, I will hurt him. I can't stop thinking about him. Perhaps I deserve this." In this example we see that Martha had various issues to work on: she needed to accept harsh reality and end her fantasies; to love herself and work on her self-esteem so as to understand that she deserved more. She needed to control her thoughts and the narrative she was telling herself.

These are three examples of how we let certain tendencies take over our lives; we make martyrs of ourselves and we blame and belittle ourselves. To free yourself from the impulse to stifle or reject your creative voice, to stop blaming and beating yourself up, you should be open to perceiving and listening to yourself. Be brave and believe in yourself and your voice of inner wisdom. Be careful not to give too much credence to outside opinions; sometimes we are conditioned from the inside to please others and look good at the cost of denying our inner voice.

When you have a strong self-regard, you experience taking care of yourself as self-nourishment. However, you really have to want to do it well. It takes willpower and perseverance, or all our efforts go to waste; we continue to be dominated by negative inner tendencies. We end up getting used to living with habits that diminish us, identifying with them and not seeing ourselves become happier, freer, or inwardly awake. If you don't see yourself as liberated, freeing yourself will be harder. It is like someone who wants to lose weight but can't see themselves as thinner; the effort they make won't last and they will gain weight again. Something in them benefits from being the way they are. If they really want to lose weight, they need to change their self-image and modify certain mental and behavioural habits. Let's look at the importance of self-image when it comes to caring for yourself.

Self-image

When someone has come to a more realistic vision of themselves, they don't get snowed under with unachievable aims, nor do they undervalue themselves by setting goals that diminish them. We should set ourselves goals that are appropriate for our self. We need to know ourselves and be aware of the extent to which our self-image coincides or not with our real and authentic self. It might be a question of *reorganising* the concept you have of yourself. This means that you no longer perceive yourself as an unacceptable person, unworthy of respect, useless, lacking in skills, uncreative, incapable, ugly, obliged to live according to standards of others and insecure. You will also need to stop judging yourself, because judgment that threatens one's self-image causes insecurity. This doesn't mean that you shouldn't be self-critical, but in a kinder and more constructive way, making an effort to improve.

To bring about these changes in your self-perception, try to let go of patterns of habitual thinking that perpetuate a concept and self-image based on external models or limiting patterns – these prevent you from flourishing. Developing a concept of yourself as a worthwhile person able to establish your own standards and values based on your experience and emphasising more positive and appreciative attitudes towards yourself will make you feel great. You will shine more and your contribution to relationships will be stronger and transformative. As Marianne Williamson wrote:[5]

Our deepest fear is not that we are inadequate. Our deepest

fear is that we are powerful beyond measure. It is our light, not our darkness, that most frightens us.

We ask ourselves: who am I to be brilliant, gorgeous, talented, fabulous?

Actually, who are you not to be? You are a child of God. Your playing small does not serve the world. There is nothing enlightened in shrinking so that other people won't feel insecure around you.

We were born to make manifest the glory of God that is within us.

It's not just in some of us, it is in everyone.

And as we let our own light shine, we unconsciously give other people permission to do the same.

As we are liberated from our own fear, our presence automatically liberates others.

When accompanying people in their personal development, I have observed that, in the search for meaning and for ourselves, rather than focusing on the essential questions, we repeat statements that debilitate us, such as "I won't be able to", "This is impossible", "I am small and insignificant", "It isn't fair"; and we entertain questions such as: "Why is it me that has to go through this?", "Is it that perhaps I don't deserve anything better?", "When will you change?", "When will you leave me alone?", "Why didn't you tell me before?", "Who are you to...?", "Why didn't I tell them in time?", "Why are you deceiving me?", "When will you stop making excuses?" These are all questions that show our tendency to be hard and judgmental towards ourselves. We live in thrall to beliefs that paralyse us when faced with the unexpected, change and uncertainty. They are beliefs that damage us and cause us stress, bringing us unnecessary suffering. A question leads us to invent a story that gets bigger in the telling. For example: "Why are you deceiving me? Your explanations are excuses, you're not telling me the truth, you're not being sincere, you're hiding something from me, you don't trust me, you are not being clear, etc." Believing these assumptions to be true, we cause suffering, unhappiness, arguments and dramas.

Let's be conscious of how we talk to ourselves. Is our inner dialogue healthy or isn't it? Let's look again at the images and words we use that limit our possibilities. There are phrases that present unformulated limits, rules of behaviour we think we can't go beyond. They arise from negative images and usually contain the words "can't" or "shouldn't". For example, we get stressed when overworked, but tell ourselves: "I shouldn't take a break now because..." or when we need to introduce a new habit or let go of an old one we say: "That's just how I am, I can't change"; "I find it impossible to relax". Those words are only appropriate if we really cannot do anything about it.

The difficulty comes when we identify with and even cling to a negative image, using the language "I can't", and in so doing make our objective impossible. When we say we can't do something, we put the objective out of reach. We can put the objective into the positive and see what prevents us from achieving it. It helps to ask: "What would happen if...? What stops me from...? How am I preventing myself from achieving that? Can I visualise an image that inspires me to be able to...?"

When you say: "I don't want to...", you give power to what you don't want. Why not reformulate "I don't want" and "I won't be able to" in the positive? When we think "I don't want to smoke" or "I don't want to eat chocolate", our desire to smoke or eat chocolate gets stronger, because with the negation we bring the cigarettes or the chocolate to mind. The negations only exist in language, not in experience. Negative statements have the same impact as those formulated in the positive, since the unconscious part of the mind doesn't process the linguistic negation; it pays no attention to it.

Everything that we resist persists because it still captures our attention. That's why stating messages in a positive way produces significant improvements in our communication. Why don't we reformulate our intention in the positive? Instead of smoking, what do you want? What will you replace it with? For example, conscious breathing, or running, or climbing mountains without getting tired, and living healthily. If you visualise the image and affirm it with "I want to be healthy, I want to run", "I want to walk without getting exhausted", you attract the health you want. The image of health guides you towards what you most want.

What we see inwardly, and what we say to ourselves and repeat, transfers to our behaviour and actions. When we change limiting, negative images and language by introducing images and words in positive appreciation, affirming what we want, our behaviour visibly improves.

On other occasions we have beliefs that lead us to "I should" and "I have to", "you should" and "you have to", "others should" and "have to..." This list of "should" and "have to" oppresses us. They are invented or imposed needs that exert inner pressure to be achieved. We end up fixated on them and don't treat either ourselves or others well. People turn up and sometimes we feel them to be interruptions or obstacles to what we are doing rather than enjoying those moments as opportunities to relate to, communicate with and love each other.

We have probably never had so much and yet been so dissatisfied. What kind of society have we built whereby, despite having so much, we continue to be so unsatisfied? Worse, our dissatisfaction appears to have increased. It is a huge question. One key may be in the fact that many people shape their life around what they believe they should be and not who they really are. **Often, someone realises that they only exist insofar as they answer to external expectations.** They discover that they are trying to think, feel and behave in the way that others believe they should. It is as if we want to be someone that we aren't.

The philosopher Sören Kierkegaard6 points out that the most common despair is to be in despair at not choosing, or willing, to be oneself; but that the deepest form of despair is to choose "to be another than himself". On the other hand, "to will to be that self which one truly is, is indeed the opposite to despair"; and this choice is the deepest responsibility of man.7

I experience wholeness in being myself and allowing others to be themselves. It helps me to inquire into the essential questions, the ones that have prevailed since antiquity: Who am I really? How can I get in contact with the real self that lies underneath my superficial behaviour? How can I become myself?

Many philosophers in Ancient Greece looked deeply into these questions. For example, the Epicureans proposed that it was important to work at evoking the memory of past pleasures in order to be better protected from present evils. Without going that far back, Appreciative Inquiry, originating in the 1980s, also invites us to look back to meaningful experiences in our life, to discover and relive them. We all have positive and meaningful highlights in our experience. We can bring them to consciousness, finding moments in our past to empower us in the present, and thus find confidence in the future. In locating the moments when I was able to face a difficulty, I also recall the inner strengths that enabled me to overcome it, gaining strength in the present moments of struggle. Remembering I was able to overcome hardship in the past helps me believe that I can do so again, and gives me the strength to make it possible. As the Jesuit priest Franz Jalics, a proponent of contemplative meditation, states: "Every human being needs to realise themselves. In having positive experiences which increase their confidence in themselves, they value themselves more, and so their self-image becomes ever more positive."[8]

Sometimes we become so attached to our negative self-image that a positive one seems impossible. Seneca advocated a change of perspective and judgment towards the apparently negative, bad or tragic. He advised us to represent future evils in the present, as a *praemeditatio malorum* (in Latin, the Stoic practice of negative visualisation. That is, of thinking beforehand about what evil the future might bring us) – not to go through the suffering these events will bring us in advance, but rather to convince ourselves that they are not real evils and that only our judgment inclines us to see them as true misfortunes.

Sometimes, it is not that we have a negative perception, but rather that we need to deal with our own confusion, our lack of trust or clarity, to work out how to manage our fear of pain. Finding inner clarity is also a part of taking care of ourselves. Writing, painting, drawing or talking to someone helps you to become clearer. Sometimes we need someone else to help us out of the hole we are in, helping us to be and to flourish. If you need this, don't hesitate to ask for it. Sharing with others is one of the activities that allows you to discover yourself and realise your full potential.

Discovering and realising your full potential

When human beings flourish, they express the best of themselves. They are creative, intuitive and generate life. They promote innovation and renewal from the centre of their being, connecting to others with joy and positivity. Barbara Fredrickson, proponent of positive psychology, defines flourishing as feeling fully alive, being creative and resilient (capable of overcoming adversity), feeling that we are growing and having a positive impact on our environment. When we live and flourish, we are connected to our vital core, that is, with what gives us life and drives us to grow and fulfil ourselves.

"The mainspring of creativity appears to be," states the eminent psychotherapist Carl Rogers, "the same tendency which we discover so deeply in psychotherapy – *man's tendency to actualize himself, to become his potentialities.* By this I mean the directional trend which is evident in all organic and human life

– the urge to expand, extend, develop, mature – the tendency to express and activate all the capacities of the organism, or the self. This tendency may become deeply buried under layer after layer of encrusted psychological defences: it may be hidden behind elaborate façades which deny its existence [...]."[9]

To bring out the desire and drive to fulfil myself, I need to learn to accept myself. My experience shows me that when I accept myself as an imperfect person who does not always act as I would like, I enjoy life better and take better care of myself. I am more able to allow myself to be what I am. When I accept myself as I am, I can modify myself. "... we cannot change, we cannot move away from what we are, until we thoroughly *accept* what we are."[10]

This acceptance allows me to get close to my authentic self. How do I know that I am closer to myself? **When I am aligned and present to myself, I flow better, I feel able to change, recognise and accept my feelings and experiences. I am more creative and establish authentic and close relationships.** I allow myself to be myself, perceiving and discovering the existing wholeness and harmony in my true feelings and reactions. I do not try to mask my experience or give it a form that distorts its true meaning, trying to pretend that I feel something that I don't feel. I am transparent.

To enable the path towards realising myself, I must also let go of the defensive masks I have faced life with and fully experience aspects of my person that were hidden to me before. In these experiences I discover myself. I become a person who is more open to all the elements arising in my life. I develop trust in myself, I accept inner guidance and assessment. I learn to live by participating in a dynamic process that flows, where the course of experience continuously allows me to discover new aspects of myself.

To achieve this, stop being something that you aren't; be brave, take your masks off. Don't try to be more than what you are. If you force yourself, you will be accompanied by feelings of insecurity, you'll be on the defensive. Don't try to be less, either – don't lower yourself, since that brings feelings of blame or self-hate with it. Notice what happens inside you, pay attention to your deepest feelings and discover that your desire gets stronger and stronger to be the "self" that you really are, to let it burst out and show itself more deeply.

Being yourself without masks means to be sincere and authentic. The word "sincere" originates from going without masks, given that in ancient times masks were made of wax (*cere*). For Jalics, being authentic means more than being sincere. The sincere person says what they think; the authentic one, however, says what they really feel. However, he clarifies that "you can't be authentic until you are aware of what is happening. Sincerity implies a connection between verbal expression and thought, whilst authenticity indicates what there is between verbal expression and reality that is lived existentially. The person you are relating to instinctively perceives the lack of authenticity and so will not feel safe or find a warm atmosphere"[11] to open up in.

Trying to feel positivity through connecting to our vital core lets us flourish. **To cultivate positive emotions, we can focus on what works and make it grow; centre ourselves on what gives us life and meaning to our being and doing.**

We also need to know how to manage suffering so that we are not devastated by it. Don't let toxic people or relationships contaminate your inner space. When they do, you start to make assumptions, thinking bad things and a lack of trust is sown. The door is opened to negativity and unhappiness. In those cases, be attentive so that you do not feed negative assumptions. One of Miguel Ruiz's four agreements helps me: "Don't make assumptions or draw conclusions about everything too quickly. If you do, you believe what you imagine to be true and create a reality about it. It is not always positive nor guided by love. Have the courage to ask for, clarify and express what you want. Communicate with others as clearly as you can to avoid misunderstandings, sadness and other dramas. Only with this agreement can you transform your life."[12]

For communication to flow freely, we should work in a state of *human superconductivity* and learn not to offer resistance, states Bohm. He compares human communication to the flow of electrons. In the same way that resistance in an electrical circuit makes the flow of current generate heat (wasted energy), communication in a group can also either dissipate or produce energy.

The main obstacle to a free flow of meanings is our way of thinking. Most of us have not developed an awareness that allows us to think in an integral way, so our thinking is fragmented. Instead of looking for shared ground, we defend our particular viewpoint. Perhaps we can come to see the lack of meaning often manifested in a fragmented viewpoint: how separated we are. This shades the collective problems we are dealing with. Many of the issues we see in relationships, families, work teams or large companies, and the seeming inability to resolve them, are because we think in individualised ways that lack collective vision. We apply neither systemic nor collective thinking. The fragmentation, polarisation and isolation that result prevent us from relating to each other in a way that is satisfying, whole and productive. In Appreciative Inquiry dialogues we look for a shared meaning with the collective reality, letting go of fragmentation and disconnected individual thinking. This is one of the strong points of Appreciative Inquiry.

If collective thinking is a continuous stream, says Bohm,[13] thoughts are like leaves floating on the water that lap at the shore. We pick up the leaves and believe, wrongly, that they are ours, because we can't see the stream of collective thought that draws them along. On entering into dialogue we begin to see the stream that flows between the shores. We participate in this source of shared meaning, with the possibility of ongoing development and fulfilment.

In the two sections above we have seen a summary of:

The importance of taking care of oneself, nurturing one's being with will and perseverance.

The relevance of inner dialogue: the images, affirmations and questions you put to yourself and the way you talk to yourself affect whether you take care of or are too hard on yourself.

The need to:

Listen to yourself and allow your creative being to manifest.

Choose to be who you are in order to realise your full potential.

Accept yourself and be authentic, shedding your masks.

Go from a fragmented viewpoint to thinking in an integral way, so that your flow of thought leads to the co-creation of meaning.

Together with these practices and attitudes, for your life to be full, creative and authentic, you need to bear other aspects and practices in mind that revolve around the care of self and other. The relationship that we need to care for most is the one we have with ourselves. We need to care for ourselves to live in joy and wholeness, and not fall into despair or depression.

Taking care of the self

In classical antiquity, the *cura sui* in Latin, or the *epimeleia heautou* in Greek, referred to a set of practices of great importance. One should look after oneself, take care of oneself, have concern for the self. This required developing a conscious attitude, a form of attention to oneself.

In the *Apology* Socrates appears before his judges as the master of care of the self. "He is the person who stops passersby and says to them: you worry about your wealth, reputation and honor; but you are not concerned with your virtue and your soul. Socrates is the person who sees to it that his fellow citizens 'are concerned about themselves'."[14]

Eight centuries later, Gregory of Nyssa wrote in the treatise *Virginity*: "To rediscover the effigy imprinted by God on our soul, and covered with filth by the body, it is necessary to 'take care of oneself', to shine the light of reason and explore every recess of the soul. We can see, then, that Christian asceticism, like ancient philosophy, places itself under the sign of the concern for the self and makes the obligation to know oneself one of the components of this basic concern."[15]

The *Epistle to Menoeceus* begins thus: "It is never too early or too late to care for one's soul. We should therefore practise philosophy when we are young and when we are old,"[16] since, as Foucault states, philosophy is similar to the care of the soul, and that task that should be carried out throughout all of life. However, philosophy, both in Greece and in Rome, clarifies the author of the epistle, does no more than transpose on to its own demands a social ideal that is far more disseminated through the *otium*. The word "*ocio*", which today is used in Spanish to mean the time in which we enjoy and amuse ourselves, leisure time, comes from the Latin *otium*. The Roman conception of the term meant the time spent taking care of oneself.

When the philosophers recommend taking care of oneself, we must understand that they are not simply advising that we pay attention to ourselves, avoiding mistakes or dangers and protecting ourselves. They refer, in reality, to a whole domain of complex and regular activities. We can say that, "for all of ancient philosophy, care of the self was a duty and a technique, a fundamental obligation and a set of carefully fashioned ways of behaving. [...] This principle of ongoing care, throughout life, is taken on with great clarity. Musonius Rufus recommends: 'If you wish to live healthily, you must take care of yourself all the time.'"[17]

"Attending to the self is not therefore just a brief preparation for life; it is a form of life. Alcibiades understood that he had to take care of himself if he wished to take care of others later. Now it is a matter of taking care of one's self, for oneself. One should be one's own object for oneself throughout one's life. [...] the movement by which the soul turns to itself is a movement in which one's gaze is drawn 'aloft' – towards the divine element, towards essences and the supracelestial world in which they are visible. The turning round urged by Seneca, Plutarch, and Epictetus is a turning round on the spot as it were: its sole end and outcome is to live with oneself, to 'dwell in oneself' and to remain there. The final objective of conversion to the self is to establish certain relations with oneself. These are sometimes conceived in terms of the juridico-political model: being sovereign over oneself, exercising perfect control over oneself, being fully independent, being completely 'self-possessed' [...] They are also often represented in terms of the model of possessive enjoyment, self-enjoyment, taking one's pleasure with oneself, finding all one's delight in the self."[18]

Taking care of oneself in order to live fully implies getting rid of the bad habits and false opinions that others might have of us. Unlearning (de-discere) is one of the important tasks of the culture of self. "The practice of the self is conceived as an ongoing battle [...]. The individual must be given the weapons and the courage that will enable him to fight all his life. [...] this culture of the self has a curative and therapeutic function."[19]

Coming back to the present day, we see a fundamental need for the care of self that was so important in times of old. **It's vital that we learn to take care of ourselves, not only to live more healthily, but also to have more harmonious relationships and establish a more peaceful and respectful civilisation, with our differences, with the planet and with all the living beings we share life with.**

In sum, caring for ourselves requires us to:

Stop pursuing the "I have to".
Stop making yourself suffer with questions that lead nowhere good.
Stop wanting to be someone you aren't.
Exercise your will and perseverance.
Set yourself goals that are appropriate for your self.
Reorganise the concept and the image that you have of your self.
Stop judging yourself.
Develop a concept of yourself as a valuable and able person.
Take care of your inner dialogue and what you say to yourself.
Develop positive attitudes towards yourself.
Look to the past for what can empower you for the present and the future.
Manage your fear of pain: look it in the face.
Find inner clarity: write, paint, draw, share.
Cultivate your tendency towards self-realisation: it is the deepest healing force.
Accept yourself as an imperfect person.
Give yourself permission to be yourself.
Take off defensive masks.
Feel positivity through tuning in to your vital core.
Don't allow toxic people or relationships to contaminate your inner space.
Don't feed negative assumptions.
Communicate with others as clearly as you can.
Develop and apply systemic thinking.

The ancient philosophers advised incorporating the following practices to achieve self-governance and live healthily:

Be concerned for your virtue and soul.

Switch on the light of reason and explore all corners of the soul.

Philosophise.

Devote time to taking care of your self.

Pay attention to yourself.

Avoid mistakes and dangers and protect yourself.

Establish relationships with yourself.

Enjoy yourself.

Let go of all bad habits.

Get rid of all false opinions that others may have of you.

Unlearn.

Acquire the weapons and courage that allow you to fight over the course of life.

Evoke the memory of past pleasures to be better protected from present-day evils.

Take care of yourself in such a way as to heal.

Hold on to good advice, plant it deep in the mind, until it becomes a part of yourself.

Turn these practices into a way of life.

In the next section we will look at how to be with yourself with the aim of reaching towards a way of life incorporating all the elements, knowledge and practices that help you flourish and live creatively.

The self and the soul

So far we have dealt with self-image and taking care of oneself. However, what is this self we are referring to? This question was important even in antiquity. Eastern masters and Western philosophers have been shedding light for centuries on the self, the subject, consciousness and the soul, asking existential questions about who the self is, who the *I* is and what the subject we are referring to is.

For example, there is a story in which an old, sick layman

called Nakulapita approaches the Buddha to look for a remedy and the latter says: "It would be good if you could reflect on the following: whilst my body might be sick, my mind never will be." Nakulapita carried on searching and went to Shariputra, one of the main disciples of the Buddha, who told him: "Do not believe that you are your body, and don't believe either that the self is in the body or that the body is in the self. Don't believe that your feelings or your thoughts are the self. This is how your body will transform and improve, and regret, affliction, discouragement and despair will stop bothering you."[20]

For the Greek philosophers, and later the Christians, the self is related to the existence of the soul. Plato asked that the soul might return to itself in order to recover its true nature. Aristotle, in his treatise *On the Soul*, states: "It is, undoubtedly, necessary to establish in the first place what genre it belongs to and what the soul is – I mean whether it is a matter of an individual reality, of an entity, or if, on the contrary, it is quality, quantity or even any other of the categories that we have distinguished – and, in second place, if it is to be found potentially amongst beings, or rather constitutes a certain entelechy.* The difference is not, by any means, to be scorned. But as well, it will have to be investigated whether it is divisible or indivisible and equally whether all souls are of the same kind or not, and, in the case that they are not of the same kind, whether they are to be distinguished by kind or by genre."[21]

"With the influence of Descartes a new approach to the problem of the soul is introduced into modernity: on declaring the autonomy and non-communication between the thinking substances (soul) and its extension (body), the soul remains totally disconnected from the body and the phenomenon of life came to be interpreted from a mechanistic perspective."[22]

In more recent times, in postmodernity, we have seen the introduction of other concepts, visions and perspectives concerning the self, the soul, and the relationship between the self and body, self and soul, self and other. In his book *Relational Being*, Kenneth Gergen considers the self not as an individual subject, but rather as an interrelated being that is intrinsically relational. "As historians report, the view of the individual as singular and separate, one whose abilities to think and feel are central to life, and whose capacity for voluntary action is prized, is of recent origin. It is a conception of human nature that took root only four centuries ago, during a period that we now view as the Enlightenment. It was during this period that the soul or spirit, as the central ingredient of being human, was largely replaced by individual reason. Because each of us possesses the power of reason, it was (and is) maintained, we may challenge the right of any authority – religious or otherwise – to declare what is real, rational, or good for all."

Gergen continues: "We believed human beings are like atoms that constitute society. We believe that we are born alone and we die alone; I live in my world and you in yours. As if we accept that being alone is the fundamental human nature, even isolated internally, so your private world will always be a mystery to me. I cannot know the full meaning of your words and expressions, and you cannot access my private world. So it is as if we are essentially strangers for each other."[23]

If we believe that we are essentially isolated beings, that is, that each of us is on his or her island, then living alone is a natural act. In fact, before the crisis that began or worsened in 2008 (and even afterwards) many people lived alone; after the crash some returned home to their parents or other family members, or banded together with others, or rented out a room to reduce costs. In any case, being alone is not natural. We are relational beings, we need the clan, the family, the team, the herd...

Being and living well with oneself requires knowing how to be fine both when alone and in company. Being and living with oneself does not necessarily mean being solitary or isolated. "There is no isolated self or fully private experience. Rather, we exist in a world of co-constitution," states Kenneth Gergen. "We are always already emerging from relationship; we cannot step out of relationship; even in our most private moments we are never alone. Further, as I will suggest, the future wellbeing of the planet depends significantly on the extent to which we can nourish and protect, not individuals, or even groups, but the generative processes of relating."[24] **We need to take care of ourselves in an integral way if we want a habitable planet in harmony for our children and future generations.** By integral I am referring to thinking and acting in a systemic way, one that takes our relationships and our impact on the environment into consideration.

The value of the self

In the West, we have created a competitive society, one where we aspire to success and excellence and handle failure badly. From childhood, we learn competitive games and are judged by others as skilful or clumsy, good or bad at the game. At school, we are judged by teachers and classmates. At home, parents also judge us: "This is good"; "Don't be naughty"; "Don't do that". These judgments act as a threat to our sense of value. We grow up placing importance on the opinions of others and their viewpoints, as they determine our value in the community and society. In the end, someone who lives in fear of failing starts to fail.

"What damage is inflicted on society's youth when it is only 'number 1' that counts?" Kenneth Gergen asks.[25] When we enter the worlds of university and work, the number of ways to fail increases again. Each encounter can remind us of something in which we don't come up to scratch. From the style of clothes, the haircut, to the matching bag, shoes and belt. Someone will tell you to relax and enjoy yourself more, someone else will say you don't work hard enough and are wasting your talents. Yet another will tell you to read and study more. The media gives additional criteria for personal failure: is your blood pressure normal, have you travelled enough, do you look after your family, are you up to date with politics, is your weight as it should be, do you do enough sport, have you seen the latest film? They are different criteria, constantly making you feel you are never up to the mark.

When we nurture a belief that we are not enough, we feel shame and guilt. Or we blame those who brought us up, our partner, work, or our education. We adopt rigid opinions that can become restrictive limits we place on ourselves. Beliefs of this kind perpetuate fear, and fear makes it difficult for our minds and hearts to open.

Many of the problems of human suffering originate in a lack of self-respect, in not valuing or taking oneself into consideration. According to Carl R. Rogers,[26] we are born naturally valuing ourselves. The problem arises because of living in a world where the care of others is conditional: "I will only love you if you..." In a world where so many conditions are placed on our value, we begin to value ourselves conditionally. The result is that we constantly doubt ourselves, feel unable to open up and love others, and construct armours and defences.

We seek the approval of others to feel sure of our value as a person. How far can we trust the other's perspective or appraisal? How do we know whether they are being "polite", if what they say to us is to help them look good, or if they are manipulating us because they want something in exchange? When we are worried about our personal value, we look for ways to measure "how good" we are. We compare ourselves to others: Am I more intelligent, prettier, better, more competent, faster? We usually compare ourselves by looking for those who are not as good as we are to feel better about ourselves. And if we find ourselves with someone who is apparently better, we try to look for some defect or weakness in that person: "He might be very intelligent, but he's a coward."

According to conclusions drawn from research into social comparisons,[27] comparing ourselves with those who appear to be better can be painful. If I look around and find that everyone is better than I am, I suffer. So we opt to look selectively, and we choose those we consider to be inferior. We avoid seeing the good in others; finding their faults makes us feel better.

In recent years, numerous books and articles have been published on lack of self-esteem and the problems this leads to. Many websites, associations and courses have been created to support the raising of self-esteem. However, we can go to the other extreme whereby, through too much focus on individualism, we become narcissistic, selfish and arrogant, too focused on ourselves and satisfying our own desires without taking others into account. We become insensitive to others, empathy diminishes and the other becomes a vehicle to make us feel good. Thus are born what the sociologist Zygmunt Bauman called "liquid relationships", those where I love you when you are useful to me, but discard you when I no longer need you.

To take care of the self is to be rooted in one's intrinsic value. It is to live from the...

- I am: supported in the values, principles and beliefs that do not limit me.
- I exist: I work on my attitudes and emotional states. I am prepared to overcome my differences and improve my abilities with optimism, excitement and confidence.
- I have: I will work with the support of my abilities and those of other people.
- I can: I work on competences that allow me to progress.

No human task is more important than connecting with one's own being, the authentic self that is rooted in the healthy core, and awakening the energy contained there in order to deploy its potential. To achieve this, all spiritual traditions speak of transcending the ego. The ego hardens, preventing us from recognising who we really are. The needs of the ego keep us trapped and focused on ourselves, and we allow ourselves to be led by our lower nature. It is a question of un-identifying oneself with the ego, to let go and be freed of the compulsive desire and forces that trap the soul and do not allow it to access the transcendent dimension, that of the other and the self-with-others.

On transcending the ego, our being is more conscious of the wider reality than can be perceived with the senses. We become aware of what is really important. We stop reacting from a defensive position and show ourselves without fear, as we truly are. Consciousness opens itself up to new perspectives, and we access the deepest knowledge of the self.

As we go beyond the ego as reference point, we begin to acquire a knowledge that is no longer based on our own physiological and psychological needs. On awakening consciousness, we discover the limits of the ego, recognising the sacredness of the self and learning to transcend it to tune in to the wisdom that joins us to all others and to the Whole. That way the deepest self reveals itself in all its creative capacity, as a generator of life and communion.

*Entelechy means the realisation of potential.

2. Being in Oneself

When you can be here for yourself,
you restore a basic order that allows
you to make peace with yourself.
Thich Nhat Hanh

As we saw in the previous pages, the most valuable and helpful care we can offer begins by developing our ability for being. Being who we really are, and no longer being – not wanting to be – who we are not. Increasing our self-knowledge enables a process to take place. It helps us release fear and move towards our encounter with the other in a more open, tolerant and relaxed way. We can connect to the essence of another human being from the essence of our own being. This connection is the most important thing when it comes to caring for ourselves, feeling our own being, and feeling we are cared for. By essence, I am referring to the vital core, the healthy core. Inside us there is a core throbbing with life and virtues. I will refer to this from here on as the healthy, positive or vital core.

The positive core is the vital core of our person, one that makes us vibrate with enthusiasm and the joy of living, opening us up to our full potential. It contains our essence. The positive core includes our competences, skills, talents and our best achievements and practices, our strengths, our unexplored potential, and our values. It grows and flourishes; it expands and finds meaning in relationships, in giving of itself and sharing. If we keep it to ourselves, it withers. I discuss the vital core more fully in the chapter: The vital core.

In this chapter I make a variety of proposals as well as sharing experiences about how to be in harmony with yourself, how to feel free to express yourself, and how to be as you really are. I set out how important it is that our expressions of freedom benefit both us and the whole, because **the future of our lives together is at stake, both locally and globally.**

So, independently of what each person might consider their "self", I am going to offer some suggestions as to how to live in a more satisfying way. Experience has taught me that I am more fulfilled when being myself and allowing the other, or others, to be themselves.

Being yourself

How do I know that I am being myself? There are some things that help confirm that this is the case: for example, when my communication is flowing, or my sense of humour is strong. Or when I am not clinging to anything, whether it be an idea, role or person; when I have an ongoing feeling of inner freedom. There are no defence mechanisms in that state; instead there is opening, and I face life as it presents at that moment from the place I am in. I feel myself when I flow, flourish and grow. I shine, and my potential is active and expressive. I trust and receive what presents itself. I am transparent and authentic. There is congruence between what I think, say and feel, and my body language shows it. I am being myself when I don't get blocked by my own judgments or those of others.

To be yourself you need to be emotionally autonomous. What makes us secure enough to make decisions and choices in a way that is more self-sufficient and less dependent on others?

It is possible for a person to learn that everything they need is within. They can learn to relate to others in a way that has integrity, a way that is not demanding or dependent, not using emotional blackmail or being needy. They can stay centred in their vital core and let go of norms and beliefs that entrap them. A person can define themselves as an individual, someone who is unique and unrepeatable, relating to the other out of that "separability", as Erich Fromm called it. They can establish with others – with each other – a relationship that is responsible and, because of this, free, rather than a relationship that alternates between power and submission. "True freedom, that which is born inside each individual – with a matured individuation –, able to recognise and help itself as such, is dangerous for the holders of power. How to control production and reproduction – of ideas, of people, of goods – if each person is free to live their life and is the only person responsible for it?"[28]

When autonomous, we feel and make our own decisions, taking the other into account, but not being manipulated or dominated by him or her. We achieve mastery over ourselves and live our *I* in a more relaxed and flowing way. The boundaries of the I become more like a membrane and less like impenetrable walls. We live with an open mind and heart.

To nurture emotional autonomy, I find it helps to meditate and occasionally spend time in solitude. In my experience, spending time alone has nothing to do with being narcissistic, egocentric or individualistic. Solitude can be full and creative. A healthy solitude is one where you perceive yourself, entering into contact with your sensitivity and emotions. It allows you to see yourself and the world, increasing your awareness and enabling you to move towards physical, mental, emotional and spiritual maturity.

To be ourselves, we need to know ourselves in the vital core that lives at our centre. The vital core is what nourishes us and gives us life; it moves and motivates us. It is a healthy core, a reflection of having been created in the image and likeness of God. The healthy core may have been covered by a dark layer, one that contains our shadows or other aspects that shut us down, depress or even paralyse us. We could say that being connected to the vital core fills us with hope; however, when we live in our shadows, we despair, we are filled with angst and closed. We can even become aggressive towards ourselves. Nietzsche said: "Your bad love of yourselves makes solitude a prison for you."[29]

When this happens, you shut yourself off in your little world and your perception becomes hazy; you disconnect from your vital core. Then you ask yourself: what would others want me to do in this situation? What do my parents, my partner, my children, my teachers or my culture expect me to do? You act according to norms of behaviour that are imposed on you. You don't necessarily comply with what others think all the time; however, when you disconnect from your vital core and your perception clouds over, you do tend to act according to external, often introjected, expectations.

On connecting again with your vital core, you enter into relationship with the constant expanding of your vital space. The questions you ask yourself change. You are more in tune with yourself. You ask: How am I experiencing what is taking place? What does it mean for me? What do *I* believe I ought to do? If I behave in a certain way, how can I symbolise the meaning it has for me? That is, you go from asking yourself what others would expect of you to what *you* expect.

Knowing yourself means that you are no longer always looking for outside sources, you are able to go within to find your own vital sources. You can leave behind that sensation of self-abandonment which can arise when we stray from our own being, our healthy core. We are so worried about others' opinions, we devote so much energy to pleasing others, that we abandon the cultivation of love of self, one that is curative and healing. In the Judaeo-Christian tradition, a fear of self-love has been created to avoid the pitfalls of becoming enslaved to the I and egocentricity. In Buddhism, however, liberation doesn't come through external factors but rather from liberation of the self. It is through self-love and compassion that one is freed from the slavery of the I. The Buddha said: "The greatest happiness is the liberation of the awareness of the I." For the Jesuit Jalics, it would be about freeing oneself from the protective shell and the dark layer, and living in the healthy core.

The dark layer is made up of what we might call negative

emotions: fear, anger, rage, sadness, greed, etc. These negative emotions and feelings distance us from God; they close us down, separating us from others, and from our healthy and positive core. As we generally find suffering hard, we build an outer protective shell to avoid feeling negative shadows and emotions – ours and those of others. This shell becomes an armour, a wall that hardens us. We repress our shadow aspects, pushing them into the subconscious and attempting to create a self-image made up of only positive qualities. In a certain sense, we are indeed a healthy core of life and positivity. However, if we deny and repress our shadows we cannot do the work required to let them go.

There are people who spend hours every day in front of the television so as not to feel loneliness or despair. Others resort to cigarettes, alcohol or gambling. There are also those who, to escape from their inner darkness, overload their schedule with activities: they "have to" be doing, doing, doing. When the pressure of the darkness gets unbearable, they turn to drugs, pills or impulse shopping. "Most people attribute these feelings to outside circumstances, not realising that the dark aspects are coming from within. The circumstances are the trigger, rather than the cause."[30]

To know oneself it is necessary to create spaces in which there is nothing planned, to be receptive and available to what emerges from within and without. It requires an effort of introspection to see our inner selves. The first step to bringing harmony to any discord is to communicate with ourselves. Watch yourself: what is happening to you, how do you feel, who is in charge of your mind? Look at yourself without blaming others. Observe this moment and describe what you feel. You can write it down. Don't evade yourself forever. Trust that there is a healthy core within you through which you can not only come to know who you are, but you can know who you are in relation to God, who God is in you, and feel Him, His unconditional love.

Ask yourself: what will happen to me if I don't push solitude and passivity away as something undesirable, but rather allow for a space to go within? What would happen if I keep some periods for myself that are free of obligations, which allow an empty space to listen to myself, to allow what seeks to be born in me to come to the surface? What would be generated in me if I kept some spaces free in my schedule to be available? Available to myself and whatever might want to manifest in my life. In allowing ourselves spaces that are empty of activity, we awaken from the social hypnosis which has made us confuse the fabric of our obligations with life itself, as Alan Watts put it.

It is not just a question of leaving spaces in our diary, but also of knowing how to handle that empty space in our lives. An inner emptiness, and perhaps a lack of meaning, drives the way we relate to each other and we often seek to hide that emptiness with love and power. We are attracted to love. We are attracted to power. Without realising, we fall into the trap of a love that isn't love but desire, and a power that is not power but greed. In greed, one cannot let go of one's possessions and the heart remains closed. Craving power makes us want to impose our will and be at the centre of all plans. We become egocentric. You know this is happening to you when you end up being the central point of reference for everything: when everything depends on you, you're at the centre of the world and only you can put things right. You close off and are not open to either sharing or receiving. Disappointment is never far off when you live like that, if it hasn't already arrived.

We try to compensate for our deficiencies through physical means or sensorial experiences (sex without intimacy, drink, drugs and other externalised and expansive forms that generate dependencies in us). In following those impulses the void is perpetuated; you hurt yourself and others, and your resources and those of others are wasted. Some people try to fill their inner emptiness by shopping, consuming and distracting themselves.

The spaces we live in are getting smaller and smaller, crammed with things, with stuff. The spaces are small not only on a physical level but also on an inner one: we have no space left to think or feel from our being. We go round and round what we already know, think and feel: complaints, worries and more desires.

The manager of the department of decoration and furniture of a large chain commented to me that he saw the same people come in every week, taking away bags full of objects and wondered where they put them. He was witness to their compulsive shopping.

Once, a man rang into the radio programme I contribute to on the day we dealt with the topic of addiction to new things. He said: "My wife needs to buy herself new clothes every week – is this normal? The clothes no longer fit in our wardrobes."

This is an addiction to shopping out of boredom, unhappiness with oneself, obsession with the body, to "kill" time and impress and please someone else. One spends irresponsibly and lives superficially, taking care of the external image rather than the essence of being. It is using time to distract oneself, not to build creatively. We are controlled by our desires. If we felt death close, if these were our last days, surely we would devote ourselves to something more essential and meaningful.

A concerned woman told me about how her children were always asking her to buy the newest brands of biscuits, yoghurts, etc. They look new, but the products are the same as always. What changes is the wrappers. Her children get these products, which then stay in the fridge. The woman wonders what to do with them. They are insistent, driven by desires, taken in by novel packaging.

We live in a culture of having, chasing after achievements, power, possessions, people, objects and fashions. We reach a point where we don't know what we are pursuing nor its meaning; we live in a state of permanent dissatisfaction.

As long as the mind is saturated with thoughts, with desires of possession and ambitions of power, there is no space for inspiration or creativity. If we carry on living from the outside in, looking to be filled from the exterior, we continue to be puppets of our desires and external stimuli. When we create and live from the inside out, we find meaning and significance in our being and doing. On filling our life with meaning, we feel more whole. We need an inner space that allows a flow of curative and healing energy. We need silence to create, to communicate, to truly connect to ourselves and the other.

"Only when a human being has understood what their material possessions are do they stop having illusions about them. They know that their soul is above these things and they free themselves from their attachments. It is a sad misery to stay attached to things that are less than us."[31]

Living from the inside out doesn't mean closing oneself to the outside, but rather living connected to your inner compass, your values and what moves you, what is life-giving and leads you to fulfilment. If you try to maintain some kind of *status quo* because it gives you privileges, a position, you come to feel that because of that status you are someone of consequence in the eyes of others: that everything you possess makes you who you are. You cling on to this, you close yourself to many possibilities, and you stop flowing. We live in the snares of our identity. It is possible to construct and live your identity through what you have: your privileges, properties, prizes, position, possessions, financial power, purchasing power, male power, female power, body power and the power to dominate. If you cling to these Ps, you entrap yourself into a never-ending spiral of desires. This also arises out of the craving for fame that feeds a hunger for recognition, praise, prestige, a need to "be someone". If you let go, you open up. If you open up, you allow a flow that is always new and changing. In that river of situations and events, you allow for what is new, fresh and attractive. To let go, you need to be rooted in your healthy, vital and positive core. Living from the core gives us the confidence to throw ourselves into what, at first, appears to be an abyss of emptiness.

When we have been filling ourselves with the dependencies mentioned above – the Ps – after we stop relating out of attachment, we can feel dizzy. It is not about leaving things, privileges or possessions, but rather changing our way of relating to them, and our identity, so that it isn't based on them. Our curiosity for the new and an adventurous spirit can help to spur us on in this. The neurologist Emrah Cüzel explains how "with the perception of the new the brain frees a lot of dopamine, it connects that discovery to the sensation that it will find a reward there. If it was not so, man would never have ventured to come out of the cave. Columbus would never have looked for a new sailing route and we would not be contemplating flying to Mars."[32]

It also helps to understand the significance of the beatitudes and history of the rich young man (Mark 10:17-23) who wants eternal life. He explains to Jesus that he already follows the commandments, but Jesus tells him to sell everything and follow him. The young man's heart sinks. The commandments are about living wisely in this world. But Jesus offers him more and asks more of him. He asks him to renounce his possessions and wealth. He knows that the experience of the void will lead him to new perspectives through his renunciation, to living in His presence. By shedding everything that is not essential he can manifest what he really is. It is about learning to make use of the things of the world, without clinging to them. That way one can live in equanimity in wealth and poverty; in health and sickness; in the longevity and brevity of life. It is not about detaching oneself, not about a rejection of life, which causes indifference and no fear of death, but rather the joy of living and loving life.

In the beatitudes, Jesus shares the happiness of being empty in order to be full of God. We find them in Matthew 5:3-12 and in Luke 6:20-23. The version below is taken from Matthew 5 as translated in the New International Version of the Holy Bible as:

[…]

3. Blessed are the poor in spirit, for theirs is the kingdom of heaven.

4. Blessed are those who mourn, for they will be comforted.

5. Blessed are the meek, for they will inherit the earth.

6. Blessed are those who hunger and thirst for righteousness, for they will be filled.

7. Blessed are the merciful, for they will be shown mercy.

8. Blessed are the pure in heart, for they will see God.

9. Blessed are the peacemakers, for they will be called sons of God.

10. Blessed are those who are persecuted because of righteousness, for theirs is the kingdom of heaven.

11. Blessed are you when people insult you, persecute you and falsely say all kinds of evil against you because you follow me.

12. Rejoice and be glad, because great is your reward in heaven, for in the same way they persecuted the prophets who were before you.

Being in your body

For many of us, time passes and we are unaware of being in our body, to the point that sometimes we don't even feel it. We live more in our head. Despite it being so simple to be here in your body, it seems as if it is one of the hardest things to achieve. For example, you get up after writing or chatting online or watching television, and suddenly you realise that your leg has gone to sleep. You hadn't noticed. And sometimes you are not where you are; you might be driving on the motorway, absorbed in worries, and pass your exit, or you might miss your stop on a train or bus. You are lost in your thoughts and they take you some place other than your body. Neither do you realise you are breathing. You don't respond to the signals your body is giving you.

Although we might not be aware of it, our history is being written on our bodies. The body becomes our own trap. After the age of fifty, we see the typical "spare tyres" on many men and women. We surround ourselves with layers of fat around our waists. "After this age men's bellies begin to expand and they lose their hair, they get fat and go bald," observes Sergio Sinay.[33] "As if it were part of the male identity to abandon the machine once certain work, professional or personal goals (a position, a marriage, etc.) have been reached. Or they stop taking care of it once they feel that those achievements are relative or non-existent. [...]. How can we liberate our awareness without freeing our bodies?"

"We put our body," Sergio Sinay continues, referring to men, "into work and our relationships as if it wasn't ours, but someone else's. It is alien to us. We use it as if it were armour, keeping and burying everything inside it, especially feelings and pain. Reinforcing these beliefs, the messages we are given about our body emphasise effort, not pleasure. This causes us, paradoxically, to end up feeling satisfied with the effort, the endurance, the pain. Thus we specialise in mistreating our bodies. In contrast, women are taught to treat their bodies in the service of pleasure and seduction. [...] On disassociating from our body, as something alien to us, we don't listen when it speaks to us. And, therefore, we don't notice our symptoms. When we do, it is often too late."[34]

The body becomes the sounding board of our emotions. When we repress them, we don't feel them unless we listen to the body they are resonating in. We need to get into our body, live fully in it, feel it, simply be in it, dive into what it contains and free it so that we can be free. The body exists: it lives, it perceives, it feels, it becomes aware and speaks.

Our body is always available to us, to work, fight, make an

effort, run, produce, resist, endure and feel pleasure. However, how available are we to our body? We need to support it, return to it in full awareness. To breathe, and be open to listening to, perceiving and feeling ourselves. When we begin to pay attention, we realise that something that ought to be so easy, such as being here in this moment, is difficult, and our mind wanders over and over again, taking us out of our body and our perception of it.

The body is the receptacle of the soul; it expresses its state to us. Someone who is depressed lets their shoulders sink and their breathing become shallow; in contrast, a happy person keeps their torso and chest upright, so that vitality flows through their body and raises their spirits. We can influence our mood positively by improving our body posture, staying upright both when sitting and walking. If we walk with pride, our vitality will return. Let's go to the woods, into the garden, by the sea to walk and perceive the abundance in nature, breathing in the air that comes in and out of our body deeply and consciously, giving us life.

To centre oneself in the here and now, to develop the perception and return to the body, many meditative traditions advise sitting down and centring on the breathing. The right body posture is a great help to achieving tranquillity and being awake and present. It is a sitting or kneeling posture, with a straight back, upright trunk and open chest, the head well supported so as not to cause muscular tensions. It is good to pay attention to posture, without becoming obsessed with it, because that too distracts us from the essential.

Health depends on many factors, such as exercise, moving, mental tranquillity, emotional balance, sleeping well, clean air and healthy water. One of the most important factors is diet. To take care of the body is to pay attention to what we eat. In our diet there are several dimensions to bear in mind: health; the quality of the food; the environmental impact; non-violence;

food that is produced locally; and the economy.

To eat in a balanced way, the Mediterranean and the macrobiotic diets are the most advisable. These involve eating lentils, pulses, wholemeal grains (rice, buckwheat, millet, quinoa), fresh fruit and vegetables and dried fruits, and drinking water in abundance.

The quality of the food also matters. A carrot grown industrially in impoverished soil does not have the same nutritional benefits as an ecologically produced one. An organic apple gives you more nourishment than three industrially farmed non-organic ones. But to find them you might have to walk a bit further to the shop where they are sold or pay a few pence more, which you might not do out of laziness or to save money. When I became aware of this, I decided that I wouldn't let laziness prevent me and that I would pay a bit more. I want to know that I am contributing to my health and that of those who I share what I cook with, to reduce global warming and to boost the economic autonomy of organic farmers. I decided to invest in eating well, healthily and ecologically, and not to spend, or to spend less, on other things.

Supporting non-violence is to avoid the mass killing of pigs, hens, cows and other animals who have terrible lives in industries where animal exploitation is horrendous. You only have to see the videos that can be found on social networks to realise how horrible the lives of the animals that are going to be slaughtered are.

Vegetarians also contribute to a reduction in the consumption of water and global warming. The meat industry pollutes more and needs much more water and land to produce food for the same number of people who could be fed with a field of rice or wheat. The meat industry affects global warming and environmental pollution more than the car industry.

If you are what you eat, it is time to think about what you eat.

Being in your mind

The concept that each person has of themselves and of their "I" is perpetuated through the habits of the mind and how they perceive themselves, the world and others. In this section I will look at aspects relating to the mind, the creation of thoughts and its relationship with taking care of the self.

The ancient philosophers offered diverse guidelines relating to thoughts and to the care of self, presenting them in the form of true discourses, considering them the medications that we should be provided with to cope well with all the vicissitudes of existence. Marcus Aurelius compared them to the small case that a surgeon should always have to hand. Seneca said that we have to set down good advice, rooting it in the mind, until it becomes part of us, and finally we reach a point when, thanks to a daily meditation, healthy thoughts present themselves on their own.[35]

The Greek philosopher Epictetus (55-135 CE) proposed that "one adopt an attitude of constant supervision or representations that may come to mind" – as Michel Foucault highlights, and adds – "He expresses this attitude in two metaphors: that of the night watchman who does not allow just anyone to enter the town or house; and that of the money changer or inspector [...]. The principle that one should be like a vigilant money changer with regard to one's own thoughts is found again in roughly the same terms in Evagrius Ponticus (345-399 CE) and in Cassian (360-435 CE), [...] deciphering possible concupiscence in apparently innocent thoughts, recognizing thoughts coming from God and those coming from the Tempter. In Epictetus, it is something different: We must know whether or not we are affected or moved by the thing represented and what reason we have for being or not being so affected."[36]

Teachers and philosophers since ancient times have been giving us guidelines with which to master the mind and create healthy thoughts. In meditation courses and sessions, when I ask: "Who creates your thoughts?" everyone responds that they themselves do. It is strange that, given we are the creators of what we think, we should have so many unnecessary, useless, debilitating, negative and even destructive thoughts. Do we love ourselves so little? Do we care so little for our mental creation and our mental state? Unfortunately, that is how it is for many people. We allow thoughts to appear of their own "free will", which isn't free because it is conditioned by beliefs, fears and mental habits. We beat ourselves up, we blame and crush ourselves with endless unnecessary, debilitating thoughts.

It is difficult to generate and retain positivity in our mind and attitude for many reasons. The information that we receive from outside, in the main, is negative. What's more, we fixate on problems and what doesn't work. Our conversations are based on this news and those problems. Other causes are: being infected by the negativity of others; being influenced by other people's criticism; feeling doubts about yourself; suffering from a lack of clear objectives in life; not recognising your qualities, talents and values; not having self-confidence; not believing that you are a valuable being; being frustrated or irritated; holding on to the past; being anxious about the future; having an excessive ego; comparing yourself with others and putting yourself down; a lack of flexibility or tolerance when faced with people or situations; and having low self-esteem, amongst others.

Negative influences lead you to:

Lose self-esteem.

Limit your ability to choose freely and you make choices under the influence of your neediness or the expectations of others.

Create negative emotions, locking you into a downward spiral towards unhappiness.

Project your deficiencies and weaknesses on to other people.

Make communication with others difficult.

Have difficulties in relaxing and sleeping peacefully.

It's hard to take care of yourself when your thoughts become a whirlwind of: "if only I had done this, had been there, hadn't gone, etc." You might be able to distance yourself from the suffering and anxiety you feel in the present moment because of not having been there or not having done that, but that kind of thinking evades pain, which makes it difficult to let go of it. Thinking "if only" delays accepting and dealing with what is, creating more pain and guilt.

We have the freedom to create the thinking we want. We are not forced to think in one way or another; nobody can get into our mind, except we ourselves. But we forget that we have that freedom and think on automatic pilot. **We allow our mind to think without realising what we are thinking.** So, when there is an external stimulus, be it a situation or someone else's words, we react automatically, unaware of our ability to choose differently, or of the consequences of our reaction. Sometimes we don't use critical thinking and follow others' criteria in order to please them.

We trap ourselves into negative reactions with our thoughts. We create useless conjectures that deplete us of energy. We enter into a spiral of ideas that create suffering for us and, which, on top of that, multiply. For example, we listen to words that hurt us and are no good for us. The mind repeats those words and, each time it repeats them, the situation which has already passed is recreated, increasing pain and unhappiness: Why did they say this to me? How dare they talk to me like that? Why did they say that to me at that moment? On creating those thoughts, we are the source of our own unhappiness.

We repeat and relive situations that have taken place in the past in our mind. We don't live in the present with the freedom that we could. We allow ourselves to be trapped in our own thoughts about the past, not exercising the power to choose what we really want to think. We let a situation, a person or something else influence us and have an impact on us: an image, a few words, a scene..., and we think of that impact over and over, not realising that we are not using our ability to choose well; we choose to repeat the thing that causes suffering and get trapped in it.

The motto is: stop hurting yourself for once and for all with your repetitive, flawed and negative thoughts. Stop being a martyr to your mind. Stop judging yourself at each moment. Learn to create beautiful, positive and necessary thoughts, which raise, inspire and open you.

The history of the Mexican artist Frida Kahlo is inspiring. Her motto "live for the day" and her joy helped her to overcome more than ten operations which left her with great limitation of movement, a miscarriage, a husband who slept with other women, and other difficult situations that were present in her life. We all have situations to deal with, but we can choose what kind of thoughts we want to flood our minds with and thus exercise a positive influence over what we are experiencing.

As we become aware of our ability to control our thoughts, we understand that we can choose how to think and feel with regards to the circumstances, people or possessions that might have influence over us. What is the effect of this change of perspective? Instead of seeing ourselves as enslaved by circumstances, possessions or people, we start to be able to choose to steer circumstances, possessions or people in accordance with our positive qualities, communicating openly so as not to repress feelings and able to relate to each other more healthily.

Realising that positive thoughts generate well-being helps, because at bottom we are looking for what is beneficial. Any effect of a positive thought, whether it is about yourself, society or the world, is always beneficial and doesn't cause harm. A positive thought brings out the best in you and fills you with enthusiasm. A positive thought with regard to yourself strengthens your self-confidence and helps you to recognise and love your qualities. The thoughts that arise from your authentic being are positive.

In becoming aware of your authentic being, you are connected to your qualities, your vital core, and the thoughts that you create from that awareness are generative. You feel happy, whole, peaceful, brave, open and trusting.

The ideal is to have a loving attitude towards ourselves and the other. If we are not loving towards ourselves, we will find it difficult to sustain a loving attitude towards others. What often happens is that we don't let what we experience be what it is. The tendency to judge our own experiences prevails and we become self-critical. It is good to do this if it helps us to grow, but if it is merely self-reproach and self-punishment, we won't get very far. If we forget something, if we distance ourselves from someone, if we don't get the job we applied for, we are quick to criticise ourselves or blame others. We tend to be hard on ourselves.

Particularly in the West, we tend to judge our experiences and are very self-critical. For example, we get angry and then feel bad for having got angry. Which means that we add self-reproach to the anger. We could allow our experience to be what it is, see it with clarity and not judge it. Do we know how to see and listen without judging, accepting something for what it is? Observe that you have become angry, and let it be. On accepting it, it dissolves more easily. By rejecting it you reinforce it.

How do we listen without judging? How do we try to hush the judgmental eye? We let the experience be what it is. We can experience our emotions: tolerate uncertainty and confusion when they arise, get bored without going mad, be afraid and feel the fear without running away. We can feel joy and not chase it, open ourselves to our vulnerabilities without judgment. See emotion clearly, allow ourselves to feel it but not analyse it or berate ourselves for feeling it. We don't have to let it go round and round in our heads. We can trust in the process of feeling what we feel and realising how we bring ourselves out of that negative feeling when we don't brood on it or feed it with our thoughts. Meditation can help a lot to achieve this.

Through the practice of meditation you develop a state of inner quiet that allows you to observe what you feel without getting upset by judging it. You are on an even keel, able to find peace in the midst of the storm. You feel equanimity, you are not indifferent, but you don't go to extremes; what is, is; it is neither good nor bad. In the silence you contemplate what you feel, you observe the thoughts that appear and maintain your equilibrium. Thus you achieve mental harmony, a state of inner balance that is not affected by success or failure, winning or losing, honour or dishonour, praise or criticism, pleasure or pain. If it is, and it is cold, I recognise it; if it is, and it is hot, I recognise it. Thanks to a state of equanimity, you can see and decide with greater clarity those thoughts and feelings you want to keep and those you want to let go of. You don't get upset. Through recognising them you can change them if you wish to.

Meditating helps to accept the experiences and emotions as they appear. By accepting them we can let go of them, change them or substitute healthier ones. By accepting them you become aware of how you think. David Bohm says: "If you start thinking about how you think, you change your way of thinking."[37] If we are capable of changing our way of thinking with our own thoughts, how much potential do we have inside us?

The thought that arises out of judging and being hard on yourself, saying things like: "Why did I do it?", "Perhaps if I had done it differently...", "I won't be able...", is negative; we might even say degenerative, because it creates a mental landscape leading to a downward spiral, causing our well-being to degenerate into unhappiness. To enter an upwards spiral and be able to feel joy, peace, tranquillity and harmony, you need to have positive, generative thoughts so that emotional states of opening are generated, states such as delight, interest, happiness, healthy pride, joy.

The benefits of positive thinking are many; a brief list includes:

In the mind

You are more creative.

You think more clearly.

Your skill of concentrating on quality thoughts is strengthened, generating good feelings.

You gain more respect towards yourself and others.

You generate the skill of self-control and strength in difficult situations.

You overcome pressures and worries more easily.

You experience tranquillity, serenity, peace and joy.

You have greater resilience.

In the body

You feel more physically relaxed.

You feel more active, more energetic.

Your energy flows better, you feel more alive. Your health improves.

You breathe better, more slowly and deeply.

Your mind is in balance and harmony, which strengthens and improves your immune, digestive and nervous systems. The self-healing mechanism of the body is activated.

In relationships

You respect yourself, which leads you to respect the other.

Your relationships are more harmonious.

You have more ability to accept others without imposing your expectations on them.

Your positive thoughts influence others, you share your happiness.

You attract others with your peace, joy and harmony.

You enable others to get close to your true self and feel comfortable with you.

You break down barriers and build stable bridges of communication and understanding.

You nurture good feelings.
You smile and are grateful.

By nurturing positive and generative thinking, we bring a greater healing and harmonising presence to the world, in our work, our family and our surroundings.

Being in your heart

I will give them an undivided heart and put a new spirit in them; I will remove from them their heart of stone and give them a heart of flesh.
Ezekiel[38]

In the previous section we saw the importance of knowing how to stay with what you feel, to observe it without judging and let it pass. It is about not identifying with it. Our suffering often comes from identifying with an I that isn't who we are. We have created an "I" with which we speak about ourselves. Our own storytelling about ourselves leads us to a distorted image of our own being. We thread our emotions into the story that we tell. The emotion is energy in movement, and we mix it with stories and narratives that often cloud our clarity and make it difficult for us to let go of our emotions. We identify with our stories and the emotions linked to them.

You repeat your lived stories to yourself, you explain them over and over, and in doing so, perpetuate certain feelings that reinforce your self-image. When you don't like or feel happy with that image, you repress what you feel because you think you already know what it is and don't want to feel or suffer again because of it. But as soon as you repeat the story to yourself, the feelings well up again.

The psychologist William James, in 1890, characterised two Is:[39] the I based on a construction of different narratives over time; what we would call each person's personal history, and the I that is based on immediacy, on the experience of who we are at each instant. It is an *I* characterised by an active centre of awareness from which one can recognise the experience moment by moment.

We could say that the first of William James' *I* narratives perpetuates a vicious cycle; however, when you live out of the *I* that you are and are experiencing in the moment, you don't repeat or repress what you feel, push it aside or hide it; but neither do you go to the other extreme of expressing emotions by putting them uncontrollably into action. Neither the option of repressing nor that of "exploding" gives optimum results. At both extremes, your body tenses, your silences are harsh and your words create a bad atmosphere. When you are in the here and now, in your body, if your body tenses up you notice, and you listen to the signal. This helps you accept the emotion, but not explode with it. Your body signals and helps you calm yourself down. You breathe consciously. You inhale deeply and feel.

You capture the emotion and, on perceiving it, allow it to be. You open yourself to it; it is like looking it in the face. You allow yourself to discover it. This does not happen when it invades you. When sadness invades you, you *are* sadness. When rage invades you, you *are* rage. You lose perspective. To take care of yourself you need to protect your heart so that it does not fall into deep grief nor collapse under pain. A strong heart loves the one who rejects, insults or betrays it, not out of naivety, or of offering the other cheek, but rather with the wisdom that allows protection from the invasion of hatred and rage. If these overcome you, you stop looking after yourself and others, spreading the epidemic of rage that is contaminating our relationships and turning them toxic. This epidemic is causing conflicts and ruptures. It doesn't allow beauty to emerge; rather, it makes us attack each other.

When, with the intention of feeling our emotions, we

express them impulsively, we aren't really feeling them. We are allowing an inner emotional fire to explode. That way, they do not dissipate but rather these emotions leave a mark on our habits, on our body, on our relationships. For example, if we get angry and raise our voice, we talk louder and louder, until we find ourselves shouting. We get more and more enraged and say things we regret later. We let ourselves get carried away by emotion, to the point that we are so identified with what we feel that we are no longer aware of the impact we are having.

Can you change the way you experience situations? If you feel rage, if you feel fear, that is the beginning of overcoming them. Feeling them, recognising them and having the courage to look at them are the first steps to vanquishing them. By allowing yourself to feel emotions the moment they arise, you can see them, recognise them and let go of them without making a big drama. Without looking for someone to blame or telling yourself stories about it.

Imagine the energy of the emotion without the story that you tell yourself and others. It is an energy of great vitality, which is diminished on attaching a story to it that you don't like or that causes you unhappiness. If you allow yourself to experience the emotion without linking a story to it, you will feel a life-current move through you.

When we stop wasting time by avoiding our feelings, we have greater vitality and clarity. We stop investing in self-defence and putting armour on. It is like a breath of air that comes and then goes. We don't go with it, but rather remain in our being, in our healthy core.

In a meditative attitude, you see how sadness and rage appear; you observe them and feel them, and, by connecting to your personal strength, with your core of active consciousness, you can let go of them. You don't need to "spit them out". You embrace the emotion that emerges. You learn to explore what you feel without labelling or identifying it with a story you tell yourself. In that recognition lies a great personal power, because you realise that you can change the course of what is happening in you. In taking responsibility for how you feel and what you feel, you can communicate openly without blaming others or yourself.

Thanks to allowing yourself to feel pain and confusion, you have more empathy and can connect to the pain and the confusion of others. Perhaps you have judged others for their behaviour then find yourself in a similar situation. You start to understand, because now you share that experience. I have friends who were somewhat righteous in their religiosity. They always looked down on married men who went off with other women or got divorced. When they found themselves in the same situation, their judgmental attitude changed radically. They experienced it in their own skin, and this opened them up to a greater comprehension of human relationships and of others. They stopped judging the men and women who leave their partners for someone else. They became aware of the complexity that relationships can entail and learned that you cannot judge someone else without knowing their story and circumstances in depth.

As we saw in the previous section, many people have installed themselves in their minds. If we make the mind our home, we keep busy by filling it with worries, anxiety, frustrations, anger, and endless thoughts that agitate and become triggers for us. Thus, we bury our true heart, the heart of the spirit. Thoughts turn into a fog preventing us from seeing and feeling clearly. As these habits of thinking in an accelerated way strengthen, the mind stays busy and reactive and our heart empties and stays hungry for the fresh air of love.

Other people have left their hearts in order to reside not in their mind, but in their intellect: they need to understand everything, analyse, question, justify, reason, conceptualise, see and touch it. In the end, their heart stops feeling, stifled by so much analysis and reasoning. These people find it difficult to transcend conceptualisation and words to enter into the realm of silence, perceiving and feeling beyond concepts and beliefs.

A third group of people reside neither in their mind nor intellect, but in their habits. They react automatically without thinking or reasoning. Habits rule their lives. Their past carries such weight that they live situations and relationships according to the habits acquired along the way. They are trapped in the prison of their past. Their heart stops being joyful, since they live in a present limited by their past. Their personal history weighs so heavily that their heart stops living in the present, as if afflicted and hungry for the oxygen of love.

To reside in the heart of being and live life out of that central space is to live awakened and aware of the reality that we are not our thoughts, our beliefs, our reasoning, or our habits. The awakened being is one who is aware that we are spiritual beings having a physical experience, and not physical beings trying to have a spiritual experience.

As you practise living with feeling, you realise that relationships, actions, work, money and your body flow with what arises and that you are happier, you are at peace with yourself and act out of your inner power. You are centred. As for feeling, you observe and listen more and better, and in doing so, you feel more. You become more sensitive and pick up more. You stop living on automatic pilot, focused on "I have to do…, I have to…, I have to…" and enjoy living and the things you experience more. Your gaze is more appreciative.

You see and listen with your eyes and ears well and truly open. However, if you do so in a critical way, in the end you begin to see and hear what isn't working well, what isn't good for you, what you don't like, what you think should be different. This awakens rage, resistance and unhappiness. To see and appreciate, listen and value does not mean to deny what you don't like, but rather to accept and receive what is with full awareness. From a space of welcoming, you can transform without being broken or sinking, and you keep your well-being. With well-being you act centred and out of your inner strength. That way you are better, you feel better and everything is better.

The heart is wise. The wisdom of the heart guides us to live without causing harm. Its nature isn't violent. We have such potential love and wisdom at the heart of our being that we can heal the planet. To do so we should awaken the potential in our heart so that the full manifestation of love takes place; as the psychologist Peter Schellenbaum says: "Love bursts spontaneously into our life as soon as our resistance to it disappears."[40]

The awakened heart intuits, feels and understands the other. It sees the essential, although it is invisible to the eyes. It doesn't need reasoning or logical justifications. It knows what it is. To live with an open heart is to live with joy and vitality, without anguish or anxiety. It is to be open and generous. It is to have a big heart that shares and radiates the best of itself and of beyond itself. It is connected to the supreme presence of love, compassion and peace, and radiates them. It is an innocent and contented heart. It is clean and honest. You too have this heart. Awaken it and live it. Your life will turn around and you will be an instrument in bringing light to the world. I understand the light as the wisdom that eliminates ignorance, the clarity that dissipates the shadows of falsehood. I am not referring to the saviour who saves everyone with His light, but rather how, in each encounter with someone, you can inspire, give, raise, question and transform.

Living centred and rooted in your vital core allows for compassion to surface. A compassionate heart is attentive, considerate in the other's presence; it recognises and sees the other. Each one of its words, thoughts and actions can bring about a miracle. A word can open a door to opportunity, a thought can transform a tense atmosphere into one of respect, an action can save a life. A compassionate heart loves out of understanding, it forgives and does not bear a grudge. It lets go of the past and is grateful for the present. It is strong, accepting suffering and living the path that gives it relief in wholeness. It is a heart that lives in gratitude. It is grateful to be alive. Celebrate it. Share this celebration and let's celebrate together.

Perhaps it is difficult to achieve this straight away in all areas of life, but we can begin by changing our unhappiness in one aspect of our day-to-day life, and little by little we will create the habit of living rooted in our positive vital centre. Let's look at two examples. On leaving an office meeting, the manager says to Amanda: "You were very passive and apathetic. I didn't see that you were at all interested or involved." Amanda's first reply could be: "That's not true, you are wrong, I did show an interest, you always see things in the wrong way, etc." That is a defensive response, prepared to attack. If Amanda centres herself in her vital core, she can respond: "I respect your view, that is your perspective, thank you for sharing it. What does showing an interest mean to you?" This way, instead of entering directly into conflict, there is a chance to initiate a dialogue to clarify their differing points of view. Perhaps for Amanda being interested is to listen and be silent, and for the manager it is to talk, debate and argue. It is very easy to enter into conflict because of little things. We feel verbally attacked, insulted; we perceive that we are being criticised and leap to the defensive and conflict begins.

In a meeting that I organised at the Milagro Sanctuary, in the province of Lleida, the Benedictine monk Ramón Ribera shared with us that in his professional career as a theologian, writer and teacher he had been strongly criticised. At a given moment in his life he changed his perspective and began to be grateful for the criticism. "Thanks to it I realise where my limits are. When the other shows them to me, I can be aware of what I still have left to work on in my personal growth. If it wasn't for the criticism,

I wouldn't have realised. I am thankful."

An awakened heart feels and receives what it feels. It transcends feelings that don't benefit it. It acts with determination and courage. It moves with the sureness of knowing what it is and what it does in the world. Its lifestyle is simple; it does not need grand things to be satisfied. It knows that satisfaction comes from doing good work, from non-violence, compassionate listening and appropriate talking. It knows and is satisfied. Its behaviour reflects the wisdom of its being. It is an honest heart. Deception and lies do not form part of its being nor its life. It is transparent. It is what it is and doesn't pretend to be something else. At heart, it is authentic. It has emptied itself of the mixtures of grudges and disappointments, of accusations and blame.

In sum, **to feel is to experience and become aware of your bodily sensations, your emotions, your thoughts, the images that pass through your mind and what you tell yourself connected to what you feel. Once you perceive and feel it fully, you can let go of it, and doing so frees you.** You don't retain it in your body or your mind.

It is a question of not clinging to it nor trying to justify it or manipulate it in any way. On letting go of it, you are open to being present to what arises in the following instant. If you continue to cling, you live in the previous moment, not present in the here and now. Living at the centre of your being, in your heart, you are here, awake and connected to your inner wisdom, which allows you to embrace, receive, be compassionate and transcend. To live in your heart is to live in your vital core.

The vital core

Being and living at the heart of your being is to be at your centre, at your axis and to live and feel your vital core, named in Appreciative Inquiry as the *positive core*. I refer to this core as the healthy, positive and vital core, without distinction. It is what we yearn to live, what we most seek, and it is already within us.

In our inner space a core throbs that is full of life and virtues. The positive core is the vital centre of our person; it is what makes us vibrate with enthusiasm and the joy of living, opening us to our full potential. It contains our essence and includes our competences, abilities, talents and our best achievements and practices, our strengths, unexplored potential, and our values. It is a core that grows and flourishes; it expands and finds meaning in relationships, on giving itself and sharing. If we keep it to ourselves, we wither.

Metaphorically, we could say that the positive core is the seed that turns into the sap that gives life to all living systems; it is the blood that circulates round the body of the system of our relationships and interactions. With Appreciative Inquiry[41] we detect what forms part of the sap, the blood, and it strengthens our organs, giving us life and nourishing us. We also achieve this through contemplative meditation. When you live in your vital core, you access your healing and creative capacity.

Norman Cousins, member of the faculty of the School of Medicine at the University of California in Los Angeles, suggests that beyond the central nervous system, the hormonal system and the immune system, there are another two systems that have not been taken into account conventionally, but which should be recognised as essential in the correct functioning of the human being: the healing system and the belief system. Cousins argues that the two work together: "The healing system is the way the body mobilizes all its resources to combat disease. The belief system is often the activator of the healing system."[42]

"Using himself as a living laboratory, Cousins has movingly described how the management of his own anticipatory reality allowed him to overcome a life-threatening illness that specialists did not believe to be reversible and then, some years later, to again apply the same mental processes in his recovery from an acute heart attack: 'What were the basic ideas involved in that recovery? [...] Hope, faith, love, will to live, cheerfulness, humor, creativity, playfulness, confidence, great expectations – all these, I believed, had therapeutic value.' In the end, argues Cousins, the greatest value of the placebo is that it tells us that indeed positive imagery can and often does awaken the body to its own self-healing powers."[43] Producing positive images can awaken the body to its own self-healing powers, and it often does so.

We have a great inner wealth, a fount full of values, potential, talent and virtues. To take care of ourselves well, we should connect to our vital core and to that of others. From there we shine and all our loving and caring being emerges.

Everyone's vital and positive core is similar. It is not that there are some whose is better than another's, but rather that what differentiates us is the intention with which we act, the capacity to express it in the world and our appreciative intelligence to make it grow and expand. The essence of the vital core links us because it is our connection to life. However, in some people it is more covered over than in others. Their protective shell is thicker (see pages 30-31 on the shell).

When the vital core is your point of reference, you can take better care of yourself and others. You become appreciative of aspects of the other, such as their communication style, how they make you feel and their personal qualities. You get closer to the other and allow them to get closer to you. You are more available. You are not ruled by jealousy nor do you make yourself dependent. Living in your vital core gives you emotional autonomy.

The less energy you devote to keeping up your image, feeding your ego, fighting against what is and against what arises, the more vital you feel. And in that vitality you have an abundance of energy to live fully, create with clarity and have concentration in your mind and will in your action. With this flow you don't need to be so protective of your heart; you can overcome the obstacles that get in the way, move forward with greater ease and compassion that flourishes towards all those who surround you.

Our basic nature is open, clear and compassionate. In our being lies the seeds of these qualities and we can offer them one to another. We can help others connect to their inner wealth, to their vital core.

The regular practice of meditation offers opportunities to explore your experience, to make a friend of yourself and reconnect to your healthy core. When you live in your vital core, you open yourself easily. In that opening, you experience the joy of existing, of expressing yourself, of being with the other. We will see more advantages of being open and how to achieve it in the next part.

3. Opening

Being in harmony with yourself and living connected to your vital core gives you the security to be open to what arises in you, to what others offer and bring to you, and to what might present itself in your life. Living open rather than closed allows you to grow and relate in a holistic way. Live open to sharing, learning, suffering and enjoying. When you live open, your behaviour is creative, and your creativity is constructive. Your approach to life, to yourself and others is generative. That is, you open yourself to all aspects of your experience and so are more sociable and constructive in your relationships and all your tasks.

Opening yourself to experience is conducive to accessing your awareness. "This opening means an absence of rigidity, permeability to the limits of concepts, beliefs, perceptions and hypotheses, the possibility of admitting to ambiguity wherever it might be, the ability to receive contradictory information without needing to end the situation."[44]

When you are open, you have more clarity, and one of the most complete manifestations of love – compassion – arises in you (see chapter: Compassion). Opening to any kind of experience opens up your inner channels until you find your positive core and touch it, in what Karen Kissel Wegela[45] calls *brilliant sanity*, your healthy state *par excellence*. This is possible at any time if you open yourself – you can always access your vital core.

In my experience, when I trust, I live open. Trusting brings me close to the other. I trust in my resources and strengths. I trust there are opportunities. I trust that nature, God and others will take care of me. If I live closed, even if offered help, I will not accept it. If I struggle to accept care and do not care for myself either, however much I trust, the care will not reach me. Even if it does, I won't know how to receive it. The same thing happens when you love someone who does not love themselves; your love seems to fall into a bottomless pit.

In opening to experience you demonstrate the absolute opposite of a defensive attitude. You become more conscious of your feelings and attitudes when living in an open way. You are able to accept the facts as they are in new situations, not distort them to fit with the way your mind thinks and your guiding beliefs.

The first step to opening yourself is to trust. By opening yourself to receive the experience as it is manifested, you become more flexible in your attitude towards people and situations. Your beliefs stop being so rigid. I have often observed that questioning my beliefs allows me to live open to new configurations and different ways of perceiving reality. This is liberating. When open to experiences, I am more able to tolerate ambiguity and bear a large amount of contradictory evidence; I don't feel I have to escape the situation. This is not easy, in my experience. When I find myself in an ambiguous situation, I tend to want to end it quickly because I feel uncomfortable. I have learned, thanks to meditation, reflection and listening, to allow a situation to be what it is, not to try to change it, and to wait patiently, allowing the river to go where it flows best. This waiting and ambiguity offer moments of great learning, and, above all, great freedom. I can go in any direction, because at that moment nothing is a given, allowing me to explore and go down unknown roads. It enables me to know myself in other facets that were previously unknown to me. When I stopped living in a community, after twenty-five years, and went to live on my own, my situation was one of complete uncertainty. But I decided to open myself and explore paths without rushing into wanting to have it all sorted. During that period of ambiguity, I opened myself to different relational experiences and went in different professional directions, some alone and others in association with others; some didn't prosper, but they made me grow and mature.

I realised that it is about going forward to meet what is happening instead of trying to flee. Rather than rejecting the experience, be curious. If you open yourself to it, it will be easier to welcome it or release it; it might even go away of its own accord. It's about learning the art of feeling the emotion, staying open to what is arising, and letting it flow, which means not hanging on to it; it means letting go. Some run from feeling it, others get trapped in feeling it. My experience in meditation helps me to allow the thoughts and feelings to appear, observe them like waves that come and go, without going with them. Then I become aware of the volatility of certain thoughts and feelings; they create themselves and dissolve on their own. When they aren't prolonged by stories they lack consistency and disappear. I stay centred in my being. I perceive what is happening. Perception helps me to be present and discover what is unusual in the moment.

When we discover something unusual, uncommon and surprising, astonishment and curiosity awaken in us. We feel appreciation for the discovery and appreciation that flows through our veins. Finding and living moments of wholeness, of synergy and connection, would be more frequent and less unusual if we were to live open.

When you live open, your vitality flows. On being open, you are available. You stop wanting to be something different to what you are. You live as yourself, showing yourself to others as you are. Being open allows you to access all your potential. This is not possible when you use half or more of your energy trying to avoid feeling what you feel, what comes up, and telling yourself stories that eat away at your strength. All that consumes you. It is as if you had a vacuum cleaner inside, sucking up your vitality. When you feel slow, lazy or clumsy in some area of your life, it may be a signal that you have lost contact with the wisdom of opening.

To open myself is to take off my masks. Removing certain masks which at a certain point in my life I had considered to be a very real part of myself was an experience that made me uncertain and insecure. I felt that if I failed to keep up that false façade, everything would be bulldozed over by the force of hidden and repressed thoughts. The mask gave me power and gave meaning to my being in the world. On taking it off I felt the loss of that power and that meaning faded, leaving me feeling helpless and vulnerable. However, I have managed to move forward as myself without masks, allowing myself the freedom to think, feel, express and be, and it has been liberating. It helped me to keep in view the aim of freeing myself, accepting my vulnerability and being myself, and trusting and daring to be so.

"The more I am open towards the realities in me and in the other person, the less do I find myself wishing to rush in to 'fix things'. As I try to listen to myself and the experiencing going on in me, and the more I try to extend that same listening attitude to another person, the more respect I feel for the complex processes of life. So I become less and less inclined to hurry in to fix things, to set goals, to mold people, to manipulate and push them in the way that I would like them to go." Carl R. Rogers continues: "yet the paradoxical aspect of my experience is that the more I am simply willing to be myself, in all this complexity of life, and the more I am willing to understand and accept the realities in myself and in the other person, the more change seems to be stirred up."[46]

To live open is to allow myself to question the meaning of what occurs and what is said and shared. It is to understand the maxim of the philosopher Wittgenstein: "the limits of my language are the limits of my world."[47] Bearing this in mind, "I can only try to live by my interpretation of the current meaning of my experience, and try to give others the permission and freedom to develop their own inward freedom and thus their own meaningful interpretation of their own experience. If there is such a thing as truth, this free individual process of search should, I believe, converge towards it."[48]

Let's look at some attitudes towards life that can help us to open, and their benefits.

Trust

The first factor that helps us to open ourselves is trust. Trust in yourself and your resources. Trust that people do not want to hurt you, and that the facts are not hostile. Trust in your healthy core, which wants to reveal itself, expand and share. Trust in the universe and God. They will come to your aid when you need it.

In our search for wholeness, it makes more sense to trust than to mistrust, since only through trusting do we experience unity with others and the world, not separation from them. With trust come courage and commitment. A quotation attributed to Goethe (but which the North American Goethe Society clarifies belongs to W.H. Murray) expresses this idea brilliantly: "Until one is committed, there is hesitancy, the chance to draw back, always ineffectiveness. Concerning all acts of initiative (and creation) there is one elementary truth the ignorance of which kills countless ideas and splendid plans: that the moment one definitely commits oneself, then Providence moves too. All sorts of things occur to help one that would never otherwise have occurred. A whole stream of events issues from the decision, raising in one's favour all manner of unforeseen incidents and meetings and material assistance which no man could have dreamed would come his way. Whatever you can do or dream you can begin it. Boldness has genius, power and magic in it. Begin it now."[49]

When you trust, you support your own autonomy and that of the other. We learn autonomy in an atmosphere of trust which enables us to take autonomous steps. If you don't feel secure, you don't take them. Insecurity is the result of a threat against the image of the *I*. Security comes when you do not fear your own experience. Trusting facilitates opening to your own experience, becoming aware of it without becoming defensive, fearing neither rejection nor failure.

When I trust in the other, I contribute to their feeling the healthy satisfaction that arises from their autonomous action, their choice, their decision, of a personal commitment. This satisfaction gives them some security which, in turn, allows them greater exercise of their autonomy. Thanks to the trust allowed through autonomy, you do not foster dependency.

It is a trust where we accept the other as they are, creating an atmosphere of freedom that allows them to express their thoughts, feelings and way of being. This freedom helps them; it enables them to get closer to themselves and others, and to be more autonomous.

Trust connects and unites. The free decision to trust can be placed on a continuum that goes from deep trust to active mistrust.

Deep trust generates the creation of solid, stable human connections, and is the main source of commitment and loyalty in an interpersonal relationship. Without true trust there is no free commitment. Trust acts as a "cohesive glue" in relationships between people, groups, organisations and societies. Without trust, there is disengagement, disjointedness, and interpersonal, organisational and social fragmentation.

Amongst the kinds of trust are: self-belief or self-trust; trust in others, in the future of humanity, in our leaders, in the business or family project one might be a part of. Another is the trust of others towards us.

We generate trust when we show ourselves to be whole, when we seek the other's well-being, demonstrating an ability to meet their needs, adopting a positive emotional tone and nurturing good self-esteem. "Both people and social systems are more prepared to trust if they have inner security; if they have good self-esteem and trust in themselves, if they are in themselves in a centred way. We tend to trust others (hetero-trust) and to love them to the extent that we trust ourselves and have high self-esteem. It is easier to trust in someone who has good self-esteem."[50]

In situations of risk or insecurity, you will have noticed that you have to take a step of courage that involves activating your faith and trust over and above what is logical. At those moments, logical reasoning tells you that something cannot be done or is impossible. But the faith and trust that motivate you at that instant make you able to think beyond logic. In that moment, you do what you have to do through the faith that moves you.

"To practise trust is, in truth, to practise compassion with yourself, with nature and with others."[51] My friend Ram Prakash, resident in New York, on the 12th September 2001 told me about his experience the day before (11th September 2001, the day of the terrorist attack on the Twin Towers in New York). Ima Sanchís decided to interview him for the "Back Page" of *La Vanguardia*. This is his example of how, in a situation of extreme insecurity and confusion, his faith, trust and compassion helped him save himself and others. This is his testimony:[52]

I am a structural engineer and I work for the World Trade Center as manager of infrastructure. I have been a participant at a meditation centre for seventeen years. I believe in universal peace and I do not believe in revenge. When the terrorist attack took place yesterday, I was there, in the North Tower, the first to receive the impact and the last to collapse. I work on the sixty-fourth floor.

When the explosion happened, at quarter to nine in the morning, there were 150 of us in the office. The building began to tremble. The windows broke and the metal from the walls fell onto us. We thought it was an earthquake.

I reacted quite calmly. We had carried out evacuation drills in case of accidents and we knew what we had to do, so we went down the stairs in an orderly manner.

We descended thirty floors, passing through thick smoke that hardly allowed us to breathe. We were in a line, very close together. At that height of the building people were piling up on the staircase and we weren't able to keep going down. We let the burnt people pass first and some we had to carry.

I guided my group. I have been practising meditation for seventeen years. The breathing exercises were very useful to me in helping to control the feeling of suffocation. The meditation helped me to be more relaxed and to face the facts more calmly. This made the others follow me.

On floor 33, the situation got more complicated. We had to wait for a long time in the middle of the smoke. There was total confusion. While we were trying to carry on going down, a group of firemen were going up. Seeing how they were risking their lives for us gave us encouragement. Later the majority of those men were trapped. That is something hard to get over, but I cling to the idea that good exists.

When the South Tower fell, our group had reached the twentieth floor of the building. At that point, we heard another massive explosion. The entire building felt the shock and we were thrown to the ground. At that moment we knew that something terrifying was happening. Our exit was getting slower and slower and more desperate; the smoke was unbreathable and people were shouting and crying.

I managed to stay calm. When we were nearing the ground floor, the water pipes burst. A cascade of water was formed that went down the stairs at great force. People were slipping and hurting themselves. Panic was increasing.

We were in the dark, and we walked with the water covering our feet, over twenty-five centimetres of rubble through a corridor that was completely dark and full of smoke. All the wires were hanging over our heads.

When we reached the outside, there was fire everywhere and the wind and the heat was making the rubble fly around; it was very difficult to proceed. When we managed to get out of the devastated area, there was a new bang and all the ground trembled. We all ran, leaning against each other to get away. The tower was collapsing and we had just got out of it.

At that moment, with a group of people, we went to the meditation centre that is on Fifth Avenue, next to 33rd St. I was in great shock, but happy with myself because I was able to help others and didn't only think about saving myself. I believe that I owe all that to meditation: I was capable of bringing mind and soul together. I believe deeply in peace.

I told my colleagues to be brave; I encouraged them to keep faith and trust. I myself am surprised at having been able to breathe almost normally and able to guide people through the smoke and rubble. I felt apart from that catastrophe, as if I were not part of the scene. I felt like a little boy watching a play at the theatre. I think it is the moment to look within and seek God inside me.

In nineteen ninety-three, I was also the victim of another terrorist attack which took place at the World Trade Center. On that occasion I managed to escape ten minutes before it happened.

I believe in destiny: for me, God is the destiny and the supreme justice.

This is a clear example of faith, trust and compassion in action.

In February 2005, I met a woman in India of about fifty-five who practised meditation. She told me she had never swum in her life; nevertheless, thanks to trust and the faith developed in the years practising meditation, she survived by floating for many hours in the water, tossed around by the tsunami in Sri Lanka, in December 2004. Carried away by the force of the water and floating amongst objects, tree trunks and the rest, she had faith and trust in herself, despite having no experience of swimming. Her faith and her trust gave her the strength to survive.

I would like to share a story about how trust awakens goodness in human beings. In many countries, particularly in England, there are NGOs and meditation teachers who offer services and activities in prisons. I was in an international meditation group where we worked with prison staff. We organised retreats for them, but we also worked with the prisoners. We took part in programmes for the Department for Prison Education. We talked to them about positive thinking, meditation and self-esteem; this improves the group atmosphere.

A few years ago, a prisoner had studied meditation with a teacher who used to go to the jail to teach him. One of his activities had been in the carpentry department and he had made a very nice table and chair for the main teacher of that meditation school. He wanted to organise a programme at the prison, a kind of ceremony at which he could present her with his gift: the table and chair.

The manager of the Department for Education of that prison was someone who understood the importance of doing things with respect and dignity, and he decided that, yes, they would do it: there would be a special ceremony. Fifty men gathered for that event. It had been announced that the invitation was open to anyone who wanted to go and it was, effectively, the men who had been participating in our courses there. The manager, on receiving us, said: "These men have prepared the ceremony and the programme themselves; I haven't said anything to them, they planned it all themselves."

What they had decided to do was to meet up with us, especially with the main teacher, and look her in the eyes because some meditate with open eyes, and others knew this. They wanted to have the experience of being close to her and holding an exchange of sustained eye contact while each one gave her a flower. One by one, they gave her a flower and had this eye contact. A powerful and beautiful atmosphere was created because of this. She spoke to them about spiritual matters, about values and meditation. They presented her with the table and chair in the atmosphere generated by the feeling of trust.

The manager asked us: "Do you know why these men are in prison?" Each of the men in that group had killed someone, including the one who had made the table. In that encounter something good had been awakened inside them. There is something of goodness and the divine in every human heart, including in those who have acted under the influence of and been carried away by violence. If we look at people with that trust, we awaken that goodness in them and help them access their own healthy core. There are atmospheres that provoke violence and destructive attitudes. You can choose to create atmospheres that awaken goodness in others.

This story is the experience of an extreme example with people locked up in prisons. However, you can apply this principle to awaken trust in goodness in your own family. Whether you have children or not, we have all been children; we remember those experiences. When you trust in your son and daughter, that son and daughter will meet that trust. If you do not trust your child, they will respond to your mistrust.

James vacillated in his adolescence because he didn't know what to study. In the end, he told his father he had decided to study philosophy and become a philosopher. To which his father replied: "How embarrassing, a son who is a philosopher!" James has carried his father's words like a stone for many years, and this has weakened him. He still experiences it as a debilitating force at the age of fifty.

Trust in your children, colleagues, secretaries, helpers, students and friends. Trust in people and your healthy core will emerge. That is the experience of many people who have been trusted and then developed with greater ease. Trust is not just something comfortable. Being surrounded by an atmosphere of mistrust makes us feel very uncomfortable, but when you are in an atmosphere of trust, things will be natural, comfortable and easy.

Trust awakens the highest potential in human beings. We show the greatest care in trusting environments. On occasion, difficulties arise when it comes to trusting our co-workers. Instead of seeing others appreciatively, fears prevail, especially when it seems that there is much to lose. It is difficult to take on risks when fearful and to embark on conversations to reach agreements. To recover trust, we need to appreciate and value what we have in front of us. As I explain in the book *Appreciative Inquiry*: "When we appreciate, we move forward: our mind opens itself to receive, to recognise new data and to learn. In appreciating, we feel surprise and curiosity; we discover the best of 'what is' and we open ourselves to see 'what could be'. Appreciating with passionate and absorbing effort, investing emotional and cognitive energy, helps us to generate a positive image of the future we desire. From appreciation, new values appear."[53] When appreciating the other becomes a habit and a vital attitude, the quality of our relationships improves and we contribute to bringing out people's best.

When you trust in yourself, you dare to be creative and respond to situations, people and events naturally. When you trust, you are open to dialogue, to sustaining relationships, to mutual support and learning and creative initiative. You are a source of inspiration and, through your presence, others are able to let go and be creative.

Allowing yourself to be more creative

Creating a field of generative listening gives us access to our creative potential. Generative listening is rich; it is an inner listening in which our "third ear" is alert and active. In a conversation, we move from listening by fixing on the world of objects and facts to entering into listening to the story of a live human being in evolution. In my experience, when someone has listened to me in a generative way, I have connected to new ideas and horizons, and new creative perspectives have opened up for me. See more on generative listening in the section: Attitude of receptivity and listening.

On other occasions, I have been able to access my creativity through listening to myself. Being with myself, alone in a space or in nature, has helped me access my creative impulse.

Being in spaces where creativity is manifested, seeing certain works of art or the creative expressions of others, drives me to create. The creative being rises up in me. This creativity arises from the inside out. In being creative you express your repressed potential without fears. It is a creativity that opens you up. Being creative, you transmit your motivations and intentions. You can be more creative and bring out the scent of your individual freedom. I am not necessarily referring to creating works of art, but rather to a creativity that stirs from the awakened consciousness, one that pushes you to explore freely, awakening the intuition and opening you to a renewing and meaningful view of life. Then a creative energy circulates in you, opening windows to glimpse new horizons, helping you to see, feel and become aware of your inner process.

It is a healing energy, one that facilitates positive transformation, bursting through from our vital core. When you allow it to circulate in you, you are open to your inner and outer experiences; you are spontaneous and flexible in relationships. You stay open to a multitude of possibilities and dare to experiment in multiple situations and relationships.

On being creative from our healthy core, we choose the opportunity that best satisfies our inner need. This makes for a more effective relationship with our surroundings and a more gratifying way of perceiving life. It is a creativity that allows us enjoyment and helps us flourish, leaving the limiting attitudes that crush us behind.

On one occasion, Jagdish Chander, a Raj Yogi master from India who died a few years ago, was telling us that he had gone to New York. There he was told that, although the shortest way to reach a place was via a specific street, that way was dangerous, and it was better to go another way. But he decided to go the shorter way. When he was halfway there, three or four men, robust and tall, surrounded him, threatening him. He asked if they knew the typical Indian dance and started to dance. The men smiled, that is, their faces changed from being threatening to smiling. The innocence of that response must have touched them and they let him carry on. Jagdish went dancing down the street and turned the following corner, leaving them behind. Someone secure in themselves can have that kind of response, someone who is unafraid and whose creativity is not blocked. Another person might have started shouting, trembling; they would have frozen or fainted or thrown themselves to the ground; in sum, they would have had a reaction of paralysis and panic.

Human beings are able to respond with creativity, with love and positivity, as long as they have a good level of self-esteem, are secure in themselves, trusting and clear, not blocked by fear. With these qualities, they have the power to face things with ease and to respond creatively. They also have the capacity to observe from a healthy distance. It is what can be defined as detached observing; that is, you watch the situation, the scene, without getting emotionally involved, not allowing the situation to draw you in. You don't attach yourself to it, you don't get entangled in it. You keep a certain distance, as if it were a film. You don't allow yourself to be intimidated by it and are able to master both the situation and yourself. You stay serene, accepting and facing the situation creatively and you don't let it deprive you of your inner equilibrium. To achieve this, you need to free yourself from the influences that diminish and extinguish you; those that reduce your capacity to love, to shine, to feel free and be at peace. Those influences come from the outside and also from your past and your habits.

You need to clean out the cupboards of your mind, the old archives of your being, so that no habit leads you to close yourself off or react with bitterness, jealousy, hate or fear. It helps to practise silence, patience, your ability to reflect, so that you don't react immediately out of fear, insecurity or rage, but rather according to your values: trust, love, compassion, respect, listening, tolerance, creativity and inner strength.

You can practise an observation exercise in silence: relax. Breathe deeply. Think: I am not this situation. I separate myself from it. I calm my mind. I think: nothing is permanent. I allow myself to feel how everything will pass. I let go and I let myself go. I listen.

Letting go

The river finds its holiday in its onward flow, the fire in its outburst of flame, the scent of the flower in its permeation to the atmosphere, but in our everyday work there is not such holiday for us. It is because we do not let ourselves go, because we do not give ourselves joyously and entirely up to it, that our work overpowers us.
Rabindranath Tagore[54]

To live for a time in rural India or a village in Africa helps to let go of many unnecessary needs and dependence on comforts. During my long stays in the Indian city of Agra, I often found myself without a phone; our line was tapped. So I had to walk two kilometres to a public telephone and make a call. At other times, I would turn the tap on but no water flowed. The electricity failed all the time. I realised that, despite all these nuisances, life went on. I had to get used to not having what I wanted in the moment (water, telephone, electricity) and know how to wait. If I got annoyed, I was wasting time and vitality, and it didn't help to get the water back on either. So I learned to accept it and flow with what presented itself at each moment, letting go of my expectations. In that way I learned to be happy and feel fine with what there was. It was liberating.

We grab on to endless ideas, images and beliefs almost without realising. You might clutch at who you would like to be, what you want, how you think things should be, the relationships you would like to have or are afraid of losing. Grabbing and attachment prevent us from really caring. We are not truly caring from a place of attachment, because what we offer comes with demands. Our self-giving is conditional, with expectations and stipulations, to the point that we can end up suffocating the other. Our embrace can be stifling for the other, who drowns in our attachment.

Sometimes we cling on to perfectionism. Paula made a great effort in her singing classes; she wanted to become the perfect singer. Her perfectionist mind was self-critical towards her own voice and she tried to control it so that it was perfectly in tune. So much mental effort caused tension in her, and that tension prevented her voice from flowing. Her mind kept her voice hostage. One day she learned to let go of the perfectionism that her mind encouraged, freeing her voice and enabling all its potential to emerge. Singing became easier, and she started to enjoy it.

What happened to Paula often happens to us: we so want to control and direct with our mind what we want to achieve that we become exhausted, disconnecting from our natural abilities. As a consequence, we work hard, our minds get stressed and our bodies heavy; we lose our vitality. If, added to this, you push yourself to your limits, you can go to the extreme of being aggressive towards yourself and your environment. We do more and more, with endless "have to do" lists; yet, despite our best efforts, there is always more to do, new frontiers to conquer. Our efforts seem endless and the mental stress doesn't let up. When tired, we lose inspiration. "I can't go on anymore, I'm tired of fighting battles on every front, exhausted by trying to keep going," someone told me in a coaching session. Whether you are chasing after success, fighting to hold on to hard-won achievements or warding off failure, it is often all just too stressful.

Many people take on the burden of a long "have to do" list. To a great extent, it consists of self-imposed obligations. The worst thing is that when we don't live in accordance with our "have to do" list, when we don't get it done, we are hard on ourselves. We beat ourselves up. We admonish ourselves. We promise ourselves we will do it better next time and complete the "have to do" list, a positive attitude that degenerates because we pressure ourselves to act out of obligation more than enjoyment. In fact, our beliefs put pressure on us.

The "have to do" lists and our promises are based on beliefs such as: "I am not enough as I am, and I have to do or stop doing such and such a thing", "If I don't do it I will fail", "If I fail I will be rejected", or "I will be a nobody" or "I am inadequate".

Becoming aware of the underlying beliefs that you are clinging to is the beginning of letting yourself go and letting go. If you start by letting go of this tendency to cling just a little, you will see how much better you feel. An attitude of acceptance will allow you to open yourself and see that you don't need to berate yourself for not completing your "have to do" list. Stop berating, judging and hurting yourself. That doesn't mean making excuses when mistakes happen or justifying them. It is not about an acceptance that allows your habits of harming and self-harming to continue, or for you to be lazy and inactive, but rather being clear what it is that will free you, and, with love and affection, to take steps in that direction.

"Fear of letting go of something familiar takes us ever further from what wants to happen in our lives. It violently blocks the flow of life, believing that it can hold back the spring tide of vitality by means of this psychological dam."[55] We put a huge amount of effort into trying to make events happen in the way we planned; often, life does not yield to our efforts. Paula can teach us about the capacity to let go; in her case, to allow her voice to flow. On letting go, we allow life to unfold and develop with synchronicity and greater harmony. On letting go and letting ourselves go, we open ourselves and our potential expresses itself better. We are more creative and not dominated by laziness.

Opening to feeling

When we are open to our experiences, we can recognise our shadows. Keeping an open mind allows us to appreciate and live with uncertainty without succumbing to it. When you feel, you let yourself notice and become aware of what is happening in you. This is the step that comes before accepting and recognising. It is about cultivating full attention (mindfulness) with an open and awakened heart (heartfulness). It is to live consciously and in a fully connected way, not only connecting out of ideas or from the mind, but also from the heart. To live with full consciousness is to feel life. It is to live with the consciousness of the awakened heart. Life is to be felt rather than thought. To feel with the heart. To feel with intuition. To feel with our senses open. To feel, you have to listen and perceive with all your senses open. Feeling is always here and now. You can't know what you will feel tomorrow at sunset. You can plan actions but not feelings. You can feel now in relation to your future. But you don't know what you will feel tomorrow or in the future. Your feeling about the future changes. What you feel you always feel in the present. A feeling can evoke what you felt in the past and make it present. You feel it now. When you remember, you evoke past experiences and you relive them. You remember a sad experience and you feel sad now. You remember an experience of happiness and, on reliving it, you feel happy now.

Cultivating our abilities to perceive and feel makes us more sensitive to listening, perceiving and feeling the other. Through opening ourselves in this way, our care is more integral and deeper. See more on being open to feelings in the chapter: Being in your heart.

Remembering and recycling

Forgetting and remembering are two extraordinary human faculties. If we know how to use them, they support and accompany us in living in wholeness. "What a corrosive and undermining influence is exerted by masochistically nurtured bad memories! [...] We determine our fate by resuscitation of such old memories, unbalancing our lives."[56] Choose what to remember. Knowing how to manage your memories and what you should pay attention to will help you not to forget what you should remember and not remember what you should forget. Remembering moments of wholeness will help you to connect again to the state of opening that you had at those moments. To open yourself, you can remember a moment of opening, an instant in which someone awakened your tenderness, a situation in which you felt abundance and your being flowed with renewed energy. With this memory you return to what is, what is authentic, to your spiritual origin, your centre, your healthy core. With the memory, you restore your identity and return to your beauty. You renew and reinvent yourself. You rejuvenate and your energy flows creatively. You learn to let go of falseness, masks, what isn't yours, until you forget it because it never really belonged to you. You forget what was done to you and what didn't support you, because you know that remembering it only serves to reopen the wound and prevents it from healing. On remembering the good moments, you relive them, generating spaces so that your healthy creativity can burst forth. On remembering the essential, the original, you can come to *religare*, that is, to connect to your divine being and to God (the word religion comes from the Latin *religare*). Remembering also has the meaning of awakening; awakening in me something that is latent. In my essence, I am divine. On remembering, I *religo* with that essence and it manifests itself. On doing this, it is possible to experience something akin to a resurrection: you are born again to the shining of your being. You offer something unique to others, born out of the authenticity of your being. In this offering of self, don't forget yourself. Sometimes we take too much care of others and we forget ourselves.

I only have what I really am; this is my strength.
If I have profited from a name,
A role, a post, a group or a person,
A moment comes when it all dissolves
And I feel empty.
Struggling to give meaning to my identity and
desperately in search of self-esteem,
I decide to go "within" to find myself,
The wisdom and solutions are already there.
Simply, I need to remember.[57]

When someone is going through a difficult time we can help them remember moments of overcoming, when they were able to move forward, awakening, through that memory, their strengths and abilities, helping them again in the present, as it did in their past.

When you have a useless or negative thought, if you pay attention, you can redirect your thoughts or substitute them for others more in accord with the present moment: perceive that you are here now and let go of suppositions about the past or the future. However, redirecting the thought by channelling it constructively isn't enough to change the habits arising from what is recorded in the memory of your experiences. The memories recorded there condition or influence our reactions and responses. It is possible that they have generated tendencies towards fear, depression, phobias, or habits that weaken you as a person because they shut your healthy core away behind a shell.

To access the deepest inner world, your healthy core, you need to feel, to visualise, live your being free from all burdens; it is like being born again. In the forty-five years that I have been practising meditation, my experience is of being born again many times. One is born with a clean slate, empty and with an enthusiastic and renewing energy that bursts from within.

As you grow, different experiences you have from childhood record a series of impressions on your memory, and your inner register, that can drive you to be more violent, afraid or depressed; or conversely, to feel secure and to trust in your ability to live and deal with unforeseen situations with good communication skills. All this is recorded over the years, through the education we receive and the different relationships, conversations and experiences we have. We can be reborn: recycle, transform, improve and be.

You can recycle everything you have accumulated as you have gone along. An example: at home you sometimes hoard things that you think you might need one day, but after a time you realise that you have neither used them nor are they going to be of use to you. In point of fact they bother you, they take up space and accumulate dust and you don't need them, so you either give or throw them away. In the same way, we accumulate things in our being that we don't need; they take up space, are a burden and a bother, and on top of that, they make us feel bad, they cause bad habits.

So, in the same way that, from time to time, you should clean out old things, you should also clean out your inner self. If you don't, you will carry an emotional and mental burden that puts you on the defensive, causes phobias, depression or fears. You feel the insecurity of failing again, of having that accident again, of having that experience again that caused you so much fear, or you might feel sadness about a past that cannot return. If you get rid of the fears and the associated anger, you leave space for the new: it is a rebirth; you remove your armour and allow your vital, healthy and creative core to appear.

On occasion, it might seem almost impossible to achieve this, but I have seen exemplary cases that make me confident it is possible. One is the example of Elizabeth, who, returning one morning from meditation, found her son dead in the bath. He had been undergoing treatment to free himself from drug addiction, but one morning he arrived home after having taken drugs and, in the bath, "he departed". She embraced this fact that was so immensely painful, and was able to accept and remake her life. In contrast, Melanie had been living for the last ten years constantly lamenting the loss of her son to a motorbike accident. Melanie was submerged in sadness and depression. She couldn't accept what had happened and couldn't stop turning it over and over in her mind.

With the practice of meditation, you learn to decide which experiences and habits you want to continue in your life, and which you want to get rid of by recycling or letting them go: that is, no longer feeding them. It is important to think positively to maintain good self-esteem, trying to choose and retain scenes, dialogues and positive memories out of your legacy of memories, such as when you felt loved and joyful. Learning to clear out certain inner memory banks and strengthen others is a sign of having mastery over yourself and a strong ability to self-manage. Evidently, in Elizabeth and Melanie's cases, those memories will always be accompanied by the sadness caused by the loss of a son, but a vital attitude can allow you to rebuild your life and let your creative self flower; alternatively, you can sink into depression and live miserably as a victim of what happened.

In meditation, in reflection and silence, you learn to reconnect to your inner control mechanism, which includes the ability to discern, decide, make a judgment, be aware of what is of use to you and what isn't, what takes priority and what does not, what you want and what you don't, and what is beneficial for everyone.

In that stored bank of all your experience, it is very possible that there are many things that are the source and cause of fears that you still cling to: perhaps you felt wounded, deceived, you were taken advantage of, rejected, this happened to you, that did, you failed, you had an illness, you had an accident, etc.

To begin, we should be prepared to let go and do the work of deep introspection. We can sit down in silence, in solitude and contemplation, and embrace suffering. "When something arises out of our subconscious, we let it come to us. This makes us suffer. If we can perceive it and contemplate it, we return to the present and, although the wound continues to sting, we don't worry about it anymore. It will heal thanks to the forces of our nature. Slowly, everything will get better. The wound scars over. It is there, but it doesn't hurt any more. It is about neither repressing nor rejecting, but rather accepting, suffering, trusting, loving and releasing."[58] I thus overcome the pain and can manifest more love in my behaviour and in my life. I accept and I forgive. I fill myself with the power of silence, the power of divine love, the love of God, allowing this to free me from the pressure of suffering.

Gratitude

Gratitude and giving thanks allow us to live with openness and help us to abide with suffering without it smothering us and shutting us down. It is good to cultivate a grateful mind that doesn't allow negative perceptions to cloud the view. Be thankful for what you have, what is, the life that moves you and what you are learning. Instead of focusing on what you don't have, on what isn't working, complaining about everything that isn't as you think it should be, start being grateful for what is. Gratitude opens our mind and our heart. On opening the mind, our capacity to achieve more by doing less is expanded. We spend less vital energy than we otherwise would waste on anxiety, stress and resistance to what is.

On being grateful, you create a restful space inside you. Stop complicating things mentally. If your mind complicates and twists things, creating a heavy reality, you would feel anxious even if you were in paradise. If your mind is not your friend and continues complaining in a sabotaging, critical attitude, you would boycott your positive achievements even if you were to receive grace. Some film and music stars ranked highest on the global artistic scale end up committing suicide or overdosing on drugs. The anxiety they feel makes it difficult for them to be grateful for everything they mean to the world, and perhaps they haven't cultivated themselves within, so after huge applause they return to an anguished loneliness.

The mind can become your friend or your worst enemy, creating inner paradises or hells. Being hostage to your own mind, it doesn't matter how well you act, you never feel satisfied. You live in a state of masochism, mistreating instead of taking care of yourself and looking after your own vitality. Relax.

Relaxing and opening channels

The body teaches us a great lesson: when we place ourselves in a posture, an *asana*, in the practice of *hatha yoga*, we should allow the body to relax; that way it stretches and the muscles collaborate by stretching and going into the desired posture. If we are anxious and force ourselves, the body resists. In contrast, by relaxing, the body opens itself naturally from within and allows us to let go into a complete stretch. We achieve more with less effort. A way of relaxing the body and making it feel trust is to pay it attention.

When relaxed, we permit others to relax and let go in our presence. In a relaxed, open and trusting attitude, fear or the need to be on the defensive is reduced; people's ability to communicate their feelings freely is fostered. You open up channels thanks to which you can communicate with greater ease, enabling others to communicate their feelings with trust and reveal their private world. This enriches us mutually, making it easier for us to understand each other. On relaxing we relinquish the barriers between us and express ourselves in a way that is more whole.

4. Being in Relationship

When we seek to discover the best in others,
we somehow bring out the best in ourselves.
William Arthur Ward[59]

Together, we generate the meaning of what we experience and perceive. Each person creates their own meaning in relationship to the other: who we are to one another, how much we matter to them and they to us. "It is through relational processes that we create the world we want to live and work in," says Kenneth Gergen. "We recognize that as we create meaning, we are preparing the ground for action. The meaning of the action becomes intertwined. As we generate meaning together, we create the future."[60] "We create significance through our collaborative activities; and while we talk, we hear new voices, we ask questions and think about alternative metaphors... we cross a threshold which leads us to new worlds of significance and meaning. Our future is for us to create together."[61]

Our well-being depends to a great extent on our ways of relating to each other. But how do we take care of these practices, especially in today's conditions of rapid changes, with high stress levels and multiple commitments? This question is fundamental to the well-being of individuals, families, communities and workplaces. We are all in danger if relationships deteriorate.

Traditional practices for improving relationships focus on individual well-being. When we think about ourselves without taking the needs and views of the other into account, the likelihood of tensions, misunderstandings and estrangement increases. It is important to attend to the relational space and focus on ways of fostering relationships and relational spaces. We need to create new ways of connecting with each other, particularly in adverse situations, when conflicts of opinion or values arise, when problems must be solved, when there are disappointments, blame and bitterness, attacks and defensiveness. We have to explore the possibilities of ongoing creative action in our own relational environment. Some of these possibilities are put forward in the following pages.

For relationships to flourish, taking care of each other is fundamental. We are relational beings and as people we give meaning to our being and doing. We construct ourselves together. In being with another, we see ourselves in a mirror and grow. Relationships become a process of revelation involving both self and other, where one discovers oneself through discovering the other. People are able to realise themselves more completely when they are fully in the presence of the other and able to forget their image of themselves.

We are the fruit of our relationships; we were born out of one. All our development comes about through relationships. From the moment of birth we relate to others: our mother, father, siblings, grandparents, friends, teachers, companions, and so on; everyone is the result of multiple relationships. We create ourselves through those connections. We are relational and social beings. When I ask people what is meaningful to them, what gives significance to their lives, their answers revolve around love: that is, the networks that allow the expression of love, such as relationships with children, family, work colleagues, friends and God.

Even if we were physically isolated, we would find traces of links with others in each of our actions, ideas, and desires. By sharing with others, we can learn to know ourselves better. In relating to the other, I have the chance to reveal a part of myself that otherwise might have remained hidden. I learn more about myself as the other becomes a mirror in which my self is revealed.

However, if relationships are a means to gratification, pleasure seeking, an escape or distraction, there can be no self-knowledge. You can't see yourself in the mirror of the other, because you are using them to run from yourself or your loneliness. You seek an outer stimulus which prevents you from going inside yourself. At other points, you may want to stay with the familiar, limiting the relationship to a level of safety, habit or routine. The relationship then becomes one more activity in which self-knowledge is not explored.

To care for ourselves and for the other, we need to find out what we are like, how we feel together, and what interferes with our connection to each other. Sometimes our fears and inhibitions keep us closed off. When these inhibitions and fears are dissipated, there is resonance, harmony; what Piaget calls the *élan*, and Jung, the *current*. In Appreciative Inquiry we call it flourishing together, connecting to our positive core. For Schellenbaum, it's *vital energy*. This is released in the relational space, from the I to the other and from the other to me. When this happens, we feel an uplifting force, an impulse leading us forward, there is harmony. In this experience, affliction disappears and there is joy.

According to Schellenbaum,[62] these experiences of vital energy "do not change anything, except perhaps for transforming themselves into a new, fundamental sense of life permeating our least thoughts and actions". Then there is continuous learning and knowledge in the relationship.

Authentic relationships do not remain static; they change and flow. "Relationships, like people, grow, renew themselves; they are at all times in their present state, which is not the past or future state. When the relationship is a becoming, the real commitment is towards myself. It is about each finding their own center and discovering the future of each particular relationship between each man and woman they meet. The first commitment a human being can make is from their freedom to choose and take responsibility for their choices. If I choose the other, seeing what the other is going to be, and not what I need them to be –

and I hope or demand – that it is so, I will know that I am solely responsible for my choice. When the commitment is, in fact, about making the other person responsible for me choosing him or her and what he or she does or doesn't do for me, the chances are that I will feel frustrated or betrayed."[63] We often use the word commitment to try to fix a situation, to freeze the present moment and make the connection into an object. To ensure that this does not happen, it is good to focus on expressing the best of oneself and staying open to what manifests in the present.

To connect with your source of vitality, it can help to remember how you felt during a moment of living fully. Try to relive those sensations to help you reconnect with the best of you. In that state, you are usually creative, intuitive, generating life and bringing your best to the other. It promotes renewal and connects to the other or others with joy and positivity, contributing to relational flourishing. It is a state of feeling fully alive, creative and resilient (able to overcome adversity); we feel that we are growing and having a positive impact on our environment. We flourish when open to receiving and giving love; our creative impulses break through and our potential is manifested. We feel alive and our energy flows. Our relationships take on meaning.

If friendships and relationships are so important, caring for them must be a priority. To do this we can:

Cultivate an appreciative attitude.
Be careful not to fall into expectations that become a trap.
Bring up the necessary conversations.
Listen.
Be there for the other.
Not avoid conflict, but rather deal with it through non-violent communication; when suffering arises, to be there and take the time necessary.
Be fully aware of our pain, vulnerability and suffering, as well as our joy and wonderful vitality.

Sincerity matters in our exchanges. Let's find and live the positive more often in our daily experience. Kindness counts: paying attention to others strengthens our bonds. Relationships are a source of both happiness and suffering. We find happiness in a good friendship, a good love bond, a conversation, intimate and meaningful sharing or in a shared adventure. All of this nourishes us. However, relationships are also what cause us the greatest suffering. Misunderstandings, arguments and conflicts can be a constant source of upset. Unfortunately, sometimes it takes the loss of a loved one to make us feel that perhaps we should have taken more care of the relationship. How many times have we heard that, on their deathbed, people regret not having cared better for their friends or family, that they didn't spend more time talking and being with them. "Very early in life is too late," says Marguerite Duras.[64]

Sometimes we take better care of relationships in difficult times. In contrast, when times are good, we can start to take "having" that person, whether husband, wife, friend or partner, for granted. Then you stop being sensitive to them, stop taking care of them and being attentive to their presence, to what is going on for them, and their needs. When you start a relationship, you take care of the little things. Over time, once that person has become part of your close relational circle, you often stop taking care of them so well. You don't listen, you don't spend time with them, you don't realise when the other person is going through delicate moments. **We are all caregivers and people who need to be cared for, cherished, loved. We all need to both offer and receive care.**

Care is personal; what suits one person may not suit another. You often receive advice based on something that worked well for the other. But maybe you need something else, another suggestion. Above all, sometimes you need to be listened to without being given advice.

When someone suffers, what helps? What can you do to be of

support? What have others done in your life to look after you, that worked well for you?

Taking care of someone else requires us to maintain a healthy distance, respecting their individuality while also respecting our own. Sometimes you make plans for other people based on your desires and you may end up feeling frustrated and tired. You try to help according to your own criteria. "If Martha left her abusive husband, she'd be much better off." Well, Martha hasn't left him, she has decided to stay. She is not willing or ready to take that step. She has her reasons. If we don't respect her and her reasons, we won't be able to help her.

In this sense, Carl R. Rogers raises questions that can help us: "Am I secure enough within myself to permit him his separateness? Can I permit him to be what he is – honest or deceitful, infantile or adult, despairing or over-confident? Can I give him the freedom to be? Or do I feel that he should follow my advice, or remain somewhat dependent on me, or mold himself after me? [...] Can I let myself enter fully into the world of his feelings and personal meanings and see these as he does? Can I step into his private world so completely that I lose all desire to evaluate or judge it? Can I enter it so sensitively that I can move about in it freely, without trampling on meanings that are precious to him? Can I sense it so accurately that I can catch not only the meanings of his experience which are obvious to him, but those meanings which are only implicit, which he sees only dimly or as confusion? Can I extend this understanding without limit? [...] it is most helpful when I can see and formulate clearly the meanings in his experiencing which for him have been unclear and tangled."[65]

Do what you can, based on how you are and on the resources available to you in the here and now. Don't force yourself to fulfil an idea you have of how things should be and what you should be able to do. If you have unrealistic expectations you struggle to achieve something unattainable, and end up exhausted.

5. Taking Care of Ourselves

If you want to go quickly, go alone
If you want to go far, go together.
African proverb

The practices I suggest in this book are both personal and relational. They depend on the individual but also apply to relationships. Some practices are more personal, mainly dependent on the individual's decision and will. But they are also practices in relationship. There is a very fine line between personal and relational practices; in some ways the line is almost non-existent. A personal practice is relational, and a relational practice personal. The practice I consider fundamental is to live open rather than closed, which is why I have devoted a significant part of the book to exploring being open more deeply (Part 3: Opening).

When we want to be useful, we offer ourselves and our help. We provide support and care in our interactions. Occasions arise when we want to care, to offer comfort, support and appropriate help, but don't know exactly how to do so. When we hear of a friend's, or someone else's, difficulties our hearts are touched. We might even feel pain on learning of their problems, but don't know where to start and remain perplexed about what they are going through in their lives, not wanting to be a burden or interfere. Let's look at some practices that are useful, and others that we might transform. I start with one of the latter, the "it's the same for me".

Transforming difficulties into possibilities

It's the same for me

We respond to the other's suffering in different ways. For

example, we say, "It's the same for me", or we want to save them, trying to help them to get out of the situation they are in. We may offer suggestions and advice, or adopt an "it's the same for me" approach. They say something and you reply: "Yes, I totally understand you. It's exactly the same for me. I know what you're saying." Answering like this doesn't help. Instead, this kind of response prevents you from recognising the unique nature of the other's experience. Perhaps you respond like that because it makes you feel less alone in your own experience.

We use the "it's the same for me" strategy, and share *our* experience of pain, assuming that theirs is similar. These strategies can make the other person close down, stop sharing their feelings, and even get angry. They feel misunderstood. We want to relieve the other's suffering but realise we have made it worse. Instead of listening to them from their own perspective, we listen from our own frame of reference. In doing so we cannot really understand the other.

It is true that knowing you are not alone in what is happening to you can help you not to feel isolated in the loneliness of your experience. However, in general, someone telling you that the same thing is going on for him or her doesn't help you to get over it, because things happen to everyone in subtly different ways. Everyone lives through their experiences in unique ways. Being able to feel the other, feel that they are accompanying me, are present to what is happening to me, makes me feel protected. Therefore, I consider it better to accompany the other from our full presence and listening, not needing to give advice or to say, "It's the same for me."

Allow others to struggle and make room for the new

At other times we approach the other person and their situation by taking on the role of the saviour. You want to rescue the other and save them from pain. However, the truth is that we can't take on emotional, existential or mental suffering for the other. Suffering cannot be passed on to someone else. You realise someone else is suffering and that you can't do anything except offer them company and be by their side. Or you might be the one suffering, and others can do nothing more than be alongside you. When the suffering is yours, you are the only one that can go through it.

When we want to prevent a butterfly from suffering as it emerges from its cocoon, breaking it open to ease its exit, the butterfly doesn't force through with its own strength. Its wings are weakened and it dies. The butterfly has to break the cocoon open by itself to become strong and able to fly. If we let it fight to get out on its own, it will live. Each of us has to go through the process of getting out of our own chrysalis, to strengthen ourselves in the transit towards the new.

When we are motivated and attracted by something, we will accept and endure any difficulty that arises to reach it. Motivation helps us move forward. When the snake has to shed its old skin, it chooses to pass between two stones that squeeze and scratch it, helping it rid itself of its skin. The motion causes pain, but aids it in letting go of the old to make room for the new. It is like a birth, when a new creature must pass through a small space in order to be born. It is the end of one process and the beginning of another. That transition involves suffering. If we resist it, our suffering increases: we don't let go of the old that is no longer giving us anything, but neither do we give space to the new seeking to be born.

Suffering signals that something new is being born. If we go backward, what is calling us to be transformed gets contaminated. If we accept it and go through it, the old falls away and the new is born. We have to flow with uncertainty, since we don't know what will happen after shedding the skin. We don't know what awaits us after that change, and this anxiety can cause a lack of inner strength. Nevertheless, detaching from the old, letting go of it, frees and strengthens us.

How hard we find it to allow the other to be autonomous in their passage through suffering! We find it difficult because of our vulnerabilities, deficiencies and unmet needs. "For someone to be able to allow the other their own autonomous searching, they need to be generally fulfilled in their own life. That is, to be a person who is secure in themselves, happy in their own space. An emotionally deprived person cannot resist the temptation to protect and be possessive."[66] Then the "saviour" emerges, activated by the appearance of a "victim". They become hard-headed about what, in their opinion, is good for the other. Insisting and persisting can make things worse. They want to try to fix the other, controlling them in some way.

Appreciating what is

At other times, we make the other responsible for our unhappiness. When we are very close to someone and think we know them well, we can fall into the habit of focusing more on what we don't like, on the things that bother us. We get used to complaining and stop appreciating the value they bring to us. We feel that the other is responsible for our dissatisfaction. Focusing on their shortcomings, what they are doing wrong and what you don't like about them, creates a distorted image. Their self-esteem is damaged and your dissatisfaction increases. **Let's appreciate the good in what they have been and are.** Let's value what they give to us and not make assumptions. Let's ask, clarify, be open to perceiving and to listening.

"I have learned how hard it is to confront with negative feelings a person about whom I care deeply," Carl Rogers says. "I have learned how expectations in a relationship turn very easily into demands made on the relationship. In my experience, I have found that one of the hardest things for me is to care for a person for whatever he or she *is*, at that time, in the relationship. It is so much easier to care for others for what I *think* they are, or *wish* they would be, or feel they *should* be. To care for this person for what he or she is, dropping my own expectations of what I want him or her to be for me, dropping my desire to change this person to suit my needs, is a most difficult but enrichening way to a satisfying intimate relationship."[67]

The spontaneity of the self

We can heal past traumas and awaken the lightness and spontaneity of the self in the relational space. Being attentive can help us become aware of what takes on its own life through our exchange with others. The problem lies in the way we inhibit this spark because of beliefs, internalised rules and fears. We are ruled by the fear of being deprived of love, the fear of abandonment. Spontaneity can't manifest itself in that fear.

Let's be attentive, dare to stop the downward spiral of blame and grudges, and connect to the essential desire of those involved, the longing for life, peace and love. Let's make room again for longing in our exchanges and embrace our being, which, in its essence, cannot be rejected. Let's embrace the essence of the other, the healthy core: even if they feel pain or sickness in the present, their positive core is latent and waiting to flower.

From self-sufficiency to opening oneself to being cared for

Another factor conditioning us is the deep-seated belief and practice in the Western world that we should be capable of doing things for ourselves, of being autonomous and self-sufficient. Not asking for help is often considered a virtue. We find it difficult to ask for help in this context, and if we do, feel we are admitting to some kind of weakness or failure. Some people who go to therapy or coaching sessions believe they should have been able to solve their own difficulties. This belief keeps us closed to the care that the other could offer us; it makes us hard on ourselves. Some people even reject themselves because of this. When you reject yourself, you lay the ground for the seeds of self-aggression and a lack of full awareness to take root. When you reject who you are and how you feel in the moment, you are being aggressive towards yourself.

Our suffering often comes because we battle against how things are, how we are and how we react. Much of the pain we feel arises through trying to avoid it. The more I want to avoid suffering, the more I suffer on seeing that it can't be evaded. The more I think about what is making me suffer, the more I tell myself stories and am fixated on images that prolong my suffering. Perhaps I should look further, see my life from a wider perspective and ask myself: do I want to carry on repeating the patterns that make me suffer? The first step is to become aware of them and then tune in to the will to change direction. Maybe I keep repeating these patterns because I am getting something from it; perhaps the patterns protect me from coming out from behind my armour and dealing with an issue, keeping me in the role of victim and not taking responsibility. Maybe there is another reason that needs to be uncovered if I want to break out of this circle of suffering.

However much care you take of yourself, you also need to open yourself to being cared for and welcoming the care of others. Excessive self-sufficiency ends up in separation and isolation.

Sometimes we need to be embraced in all our dimensions, without being suffocated. At times we need support to take a step forward. We may be hovering in indecision and a word, a gesture, can give us the push we need. Supporting someone at those moments of indecision can give them what they need to make a move. You can let them know you believe in them, although if your words are to transmit your conviction, you also have to believe them yourself.

You can take care of the other when they feel tired, burnt out, exhausted or fed up by suggesting a walk, for example. Sharing as we walk encourages us to get things off our chest and clarify what is happening to us. Halfway through the story that someone is telling you, you can ask them: "How do you feel?", helping them return to the present moment and not get lost in the stories they are telling themselves.

The questions that set us free

To enhance our existence positively in all its aspects, mental, emotional, spiritual and bodily, it is important to pay attention to which questions we ask. When, for example, I ask myself: "Do they love me enough?", the answer is nearly always no. In asking this question I don't free myself but instead get distracted by answers that detract from my ability to encounter the other spontaneously; I relive memories that open up old wounds of not having been loved enough, despair returns, a sensation of lack of self-worth, and rejection of the other who doesn't love me enough. To hide my wound, I justify it by deciding it was "the wrong man or woman, again". For example, when I ask myself: "Why me?", I return to the cycle of suffering, anger, sadness and fear.

Asking appropriate questions will help; creating conversations that matter and make sense will give us a feeling of relief. In asking questions that invite a healing and appreciative exploration, we generate opening and an atmosphere fostering meaningful conversations. It is about asking questions that invite us to traverse the painful constructions of the past and make contact with an appreciation of the present and our feeling now. When you try to help someone else, you can ask them what worked for them before: "What resources did you use?", "What helped you?", "Where did you find the strength to move forward?"

To care for another is to support them in their efforts to clarify their feelings and thoughts. We can ask them questions that are appreciative and open. Depending on the question we ask, we can bring about the opposite effect to the one desired, irritating, distracting or even confusing the other. If, for example, you use

"Why?" in your questions: "Why did you get into this mess? Why did you tell them? Why did you make that decision?", you are inviting the other to defend and justify themselves. They will feel judged, attacked or blamed and will close up. With the "Why?" you invite the other to dwell on past mistakes and don't help them to be present now.

You could ask "What" or "How": "How do you feel? What alternatives could you look into? What is there in this situation that works? What gives you the strength to keep going?" These are questions that allow you to be more present to what is happening now, helping to create useful thoughts for yourself and others. You can ask these questions: "What did you learn from that situation? What was your contribution to the relationship and what did it contribute to your life? Where did you find the strength to move forward? What is there within you that pushes you forward? If the ideal situation manifested, what would be happening? How would you be? What would you do differently? Don't think about what others do, but rather what *you* can do to create the conditions for your energy to flow. What are you like when you express yourself best, when you feel abundant and overflowing with vitality? ..." On asking questions with genuine curiosity that allow the other to open and reveal themselves, you allow a deeper level of comprehension and understanding to emerge.

On the other hand, when you think you have the answers, that you are as you should be, and that it is the world that needs to change – by world meaning others, circumstances, situations, projects and a long list of everything in your environment, with its ailments, disagreements and misunderstandings – then you don't ask questions of Appreciative Inquiry but make demands instead. You believe it is the other who should understand your children, be compassionate towards your mother and listen to you on demand. If they are not understanding and don't listen to you when you want them to, you think they are in the wrong. You don't ask yourself if perhaps you ought to change or improve in some way, making it easier for what you want to happen, or, if it isn't happening, to understand what it is in you that is blocking it. You blame the other, not looking at yourself or recognising what attitude of yours might be blocking the situation.

Understanding changes us

It is necessary to let yourself know and understand the other, and to let them know and understand you. We rarely allow ourselves to really understand what the other's words mean to them. Our fear of change and getting too close to the other prevents us from doing this. When you understand, you open yourself up, and this can feel risky. On opening up and really understanding another person, such understanding might modify your way of seeing and thinking; it may even change your way of being. Understanding a person requires the ability to deeply and intensely enter into their frame of reference. You may have to step outside of your own frame of reference to enter theirs so that there can be comprehension.

Understanding is doubly enriching. You become a person with a greater capacity to give. "Even more important, perhaps, is the fact that my understanding of these individuals permits them to change. It permits them to accept their own fears and bizarre thoughts and tragic feelings and discouragements, as well as their moments of courage and kindness and love and sensitivity."[68]

In the other direction, allowing the other to enter your frame of reference to understand you means that you have to be able to open yourself to receive. This experience can give rise to intimacy. The Latin word *intimus*, from which *intimacy* derives, means "the innermost". "Intimacy is the experience of allowing our innermost being to be exposed to the world and to be moved and transformed. Ecstasy is the experience of complete intimacy – with God, nature, life, the universe – but above all, with ourselves."[69]

We should seek the conversations needed for us to understand each other. Let's see below.

The freeing word. The necessary conversation.

Speaking is a fundamental element of relationships. Although to talk is not necessarily to communicate, it is fundamental because of the power it has to bring us closer and bond us, or, alternatively, to oppose and separate us. To listen to someone without judging them can be incredibly freeing for the interlocutor. We need to learn to have, in parallel, an awareness of the topic of conversation and the relationship created during the conversation. Having a contemplative attitude helps us stay conscious of both aspects.

"Expressing things verbally causes something healthy to be put into motion: the creation of awareness and the acceptance of reality. Even more, by admitting to a fault or limitation, the fault begins to be less annoying, because we can stop flagellating ourselves for our lack of tolerance."[70]

Sergio Sinay shares his experience from the gender perspective: "For men, speaking is a tool for negotiation, competition, battle, defence. Men generally find it easier to talk about the specific, about action, to make agreements, pacts and contracts. For women, words are generally connected to solidarity whilst for men they are linked to power. Women prioritise feelings in their conversations; however, when men talk, the emphasis is on negotiation. Women communicate through speaking; men, through acting. Women are clear that things need to be discussed, whilst men feel that things are done."[71]

One of the most common complaints of women about men is that they don't explain what is going on for them; they don't talk about their inner lives and resist conversations about "our relationship". "A painful silence sets in when men find that they should express feelings, requests and fears. This silence comes of the impossibility of finding the words to speak. It wounds us, it hurts us, it leaves us impotent. The silence of not sharing feelings makes us ill, causes us to explode, making a destructive use of male strength, which hits, striking out against itself or others. It leaves men lonely, it isolates them."[72]

"There is a male way of communicating that bypasses talking about things. If an authentic relationship, true communication, begins by contemplating the other as they are and I am not, who is not who I want or imagine them to be, the experience of contemplating the man before her can be very enriching for a woman, discovering everything he is saying without words."[73]

Fritz Perls, the founder of Gestalt therapy, advises: "Don't listen to the words, listen to what the voice is telling you, what the movements are telling you, what the posture is telling you, what the image is telling you. If you have ears, then you know everything about the other person. You don't have to listen to what the person says: listen to the sounds. [...] What we say is almost all lies or useless chat. However, the voice is there, the gestures, the postures, the facial expression, the psychosomatic language. It is all there if you allow the sound of the sentences to play in the background. This same recommendation would be good for the women who complain about men's silence, and we could change 'the sound of the sentences' for 'the absence of sentences'."[74]

The problem arises when communication, with or without words, is ambiguous. "Can I be expressive enough as a person that what I am will be communicated unambiguously? ... When I am experiencing an attitude of annoyance towards another person, but am unaware of it, then my communication contains contradictory messages. My words are giving one message, but I am also in subtle ways communicating the annoyance I feel and this confuses the other person and makes him distrustful, though he too may be unaware of what is causing the difficulty."[75]

What attitudes can create a feeling of security in the

relationship, enabling communication that is fluid, open and coming from the authenticity of each person? "… when my experiencing of this moment is present in my awareness and when what is present in my awareness is present in my communication, then each of these three levels matches or is congruent. […] I have learned, however, that realness, or genuineness, or congruence – whatever term you wish to give it –, is a fundamental basis for the best of communication."[76]

"When I am able to let myself be congruent and genuine, I often help the other person. When the other person is transparently real and congruent, he often helps me. In those rare moments when a deep realness in one meets a realness in the other, a memorable 'I-thou relationship', as Martin Buber[77] would call it, occurs. Such a deep and mutual personal encounter does not happen often, but I am convinced that unless it happens occasionally, we are not living as human beings."[78]

Perhaps we should open up and learn to converse anew. A key factor in taking care of relationships lies in having conversations about the subjects that matter with the people who matter to us. We need to be present and available to talk, dialogue and clarify. The appreciative approach, of listening and articulating our requests clearly and respectfully, makes a good conversation possible. We find it hard to talk when the relationship is a source of frustration and complaints. Complaints are covert requests, and frustrations are usually unfulfilled dreams and longings. We struggle to ask clearly without turning something into a demand or imposition. We find it hard to express our dreams and longings.

To encourage the conversation that helps us get closer and care for the relationship, we can ask what the request is, what it is that the person really wants, and talk about what is wanted instead of what is not wanted. In talking about what is desired and about longings, we open the doors to a generative conversation, helping to clarify what we want and the direction we want to go in. In contrast, if we focus on what we don't want, using a language of deprivation, of what is lacking, what is missing, we get stuck in complaints, neither seeing nor opening ourselves to imagining possible solutions.

In one of the Appreciative Inquiry training sessions that I gave to a group of civil servants, Paula, one of the participants, said that it was very difficult to apply positivity in her situation. "I don't like my work. I feel boxed into a kind of function and in my work there is no possibility of broadening my horizons. I lose my vitality in the office." I asked her: "What is there in the organisation, outside of your department?" We got into a conversation in which she decided to inquire into other departments. She spoke to the heads of other sections; they were delighted and offered her the chance to collaborate with them. Then she asked her boss about the possibility of collaborating with the other departments, and doors were opened for her. Nobody was restricting her except herself and her beliefs. Sometimes we can't see the wood for the trees.

In the relationship between a couple, it is easy to get into conflict over little things; a WhatsApp, a call, something left undone, and the arguing starts. Both are convinced that they are right. The argument leads to bad moods and an unpleasant atmosphere. Perhaps we should be able to laugh at ourselves and focus on what is essential. Learn how to wait to say something at the right moment and not add fuel to the fire, thus avoiding unnecessary arguments and conflicts.

Some conflicts and ruptures happen when both parties believe they are right and won't let go of their idea. They both find reasons to justify that "it's like this". This attitude gives them certainty and reaffirms them. But it also feeds conflict when the other person or the other party – children, a group, a political party or a community – has a different opinion. If both cling to their position and there is no opening to dialogue, the breakdown of the relationship is guaranteed. Opening up to dialogue causes, in some, the fear of losing security and showing themselves to be vulnerable. They feel that changing an opinion or giving in means that they have lost.

Conflict arises between parents and children when the latter want to do things that the parents don't think are correct and everyone believes "they are in the right". John gets home after a long day at work. Helen, his seventeen-year-old daughter, is sitting on the sofa and before long they are fighting. She wants to go out that night with her friends, but he says no. He's not in the mood for dialogue; his mind is occupied with work problems. Without paying due attention, he responds to his daughter's request with an automatic "no". Added to which, as the adult with greater life experience, he can give as many reasons as he needs to.

Generally, the child uses the strategy of "because I am the only one that isn't" or "because all my friends are going" or "because you promised me". They are arguments that will often not be considered as relevant by the parents, leading the children to different forms of rebellion. It is well-known that adolescents react badly to impositions and want to do the opposite of what is put to them. Many arguments with them stop when parents remember that their children will dig in their heels if opposed. If this is borne in mind and they are helped to reaffirm themselves by being reminded of their good points, adolescents won't need to define themselves so much through opposition. Even so, opposition is inevitable. Often the adult finds this opposition hard to accept because they feel that their authority is being questioned. What is that authority based on? Fear? Respect? Love? Trust?

"My authority shouldn't be affected if my son questions my teaching or my proposals," says Clare, "but if I am insecure, it will. My authority is based on my experience, it is the only thing that I have more of than my children. I have lived longer. But it is precisely their innocence that sometimes makes them wiser. We have to be honest, and when they enter into direct confrontation, remember that we are bringing them up and that it is not something personal between them and us, although in appearance it seems so."

At times it is not so much the content of the argument but rather the way in which the conflict arises. On speaking vehemently, with irritation and using forceful words that give rise to defensive attitudes, reactions are provoked. Anger heats up the atmosphere and doesn't allow for a serene dialogue. The argument is based on "I am right" and a high price is paid, where distance is generated and the bond can even be broken. It is important not to leave things half-done. David shares his experience with me: "When we argue at home, my father never leaves the argument unfinished. He'll say: 'We'll continue tomorrow.' The important things have to be ended well. You can't leave something that doesn't make sense, or a wound, hanging in the air... We'll talk about this again tomorrow. Let emotions cool down first. This way of doing things works not only with one's children, but also at work and with friends."

To open up this kind of meaningful conversation, we can't be in a hurry; if we are it means that when we talk we are not creative communicators. Instead we do it in a routine and bored way, a listless way, especially when we see the conversation as an interruption of what we had planned, when this conversation with the other wasn't part of our plans. We usually plan meetings and actions in specific places and times. But when the unexpected arises and we insist on clinging on to what we have planned, we stop listening to the signals being sent to us by our body, by others and in the present moment. We live in our planning mind that wants to achieve its objectives, not listening to the body and the moment.

Sometimes we force ourselves to go ahead with the plans that we have made and the commitments we have taken on. At other times we oblige ourselves to follow the timetable imposed by others. We keep going without stopping, without breathing consciously and without listening. People pass us or are there with us, and there is no time for them because we "should" carry out our plans. Life passes us by. We don't look after our relationship with the other or with our body. Commitments are met, but opportunities and encounters are lost. Walks are not shared, conversations are not held and people are not paid attention to. Opportunities are missed to reconnect with the other, because "we had to do" the something else that was in our plan. When we act in this way, we get trapped in the planning of the mind and we want reality to endorse it.

Aiming to make reality adapt to you is a source of stress. Many elements influence the creation of the reality of each moment; you are one of them, but not the only one. A balance is required between flowing with what comes to you and staying with the direction you had planned. An equilibrium is needed between what you feel to be your inner compass guiding you and the outer events and signals that give you information to listen to and take into account. It is the art of living in the now, so that, in the moment, we embrace what manifests and comes to meet us.

Giving and receiving feedforward

Another aspect to be taken into account has to do with being open to the *feedback* (the past) and *feedforward* (about the present and future) that our intuition, our body and others give us. To take care of ourselves is to be open to giving and receiving feedback and feedforward. To do so we can cultivate the skills of fluid exchange, of empathic and generative listening, and inquire in an open way into giving and receiving feedback. It is good to tell the other how you feel when you are with them. Be a clean mirror; that is, sincere and without exaggerations. Be descriptive, not interpretative and don't make judgments. Describe how you feel, but don't add interpretations, suppositions, judgments or blame. Share what you feel and your reactions as information, not pressuring or trying to make the other change. Lay out how you feel without exaggerating or spicing things up to make a story. Choose the right time and place to share what you feel.

You can also invite the other to share with you what they experience being at your side. Listen, and use what is helpful to you. You don't need to defend or justify yourself. Accept what the other feels in relation to you. If it is useful, apply it; if not, let it go. Don't keep thinking about why they said this or that. Don't start making assumptions (see page 9).

Discovering and fulfilling our longings

To take deep care of ourselves, it is good to open up to seeing and living out what we really long for. If your being has a deep yearning, but you haven't listened to it due to circumstances and beliefs, your body will begin to give you signs. Perhaps you set yourself some objectives, planned some actions, but at bottom your being has other longings. To illustrate this, let's look at Paul. A businessman and manager who, when the crisis hit, figured that he either reduced his salary or had to fire several workers to keep his business going. Paul lived in a well-to-do part of Madrid; living there represented status and certain privileges. The crisis and the option of lowering his salary meant a loss of his purchasing power and possibly status in that area. The tension and stress that he experienced were huge. He was consumed by anxiety. The success that had taken so much effort to build was on the line. Inquiring into his deepest longings, we discovered that he wanted to be seen by his father, to be recognised as a capable and worthy son. His father had always seen him as useless, often comparing him to his older brother, who got better results. Paul had finally managed to prove to his father and himself that he was capable and worthy. On discovering his deepest longing, his concern about status stopped being so important and his stress lessened. He was able to deal with the work situation from another perspective and with greater serenity. He became aware that his anxiety was not due to the reduction in his salary but rather the effect it might have on his father's view of him.

To discover our deepest longings, we can apply Appreciative Inquiry, learning to recover memories of meaningful life experiences, experiences of overcoming hardships, and wholeness. For example, Paul, when asked about his peak experiences of wholeness, evokes moments at which he was seen and recognised by his father and his other loved ones. With his story, we realise that what he longs for is to be accepted, recognised and embraced.

You can ask, both of others and yourself, about when you felt abundant, a moment when you felt whole, radiant: What was happening? How did you feel? What helped to bring this wholeness about? What caused you to radiate from within or what is it that you were radiating? By reflecting on the answers to these questions, we tune in to what moves us, what we yearn for, what it is that promotes those moments of wholeness. This reflection helps us to connect to our vital core and open ourselves to it, facilitating its expansion. (See more on the positive core in the chapter: The vital core.) Paul realised that it was no longer about keeping his status, but rather of looking for healthier and less stressful ways of getting close to others, allowing himself to be recognised and embraced by them, without having to prove anything other than being himself.

Inquire into yourself

Sometimes being with those going through pain and sickness makes us feel uncomfortable, and we avoid being with them. We want to, but we feel strange and find excuses to not be there. Perhaps this is one of the greatest obstacles to being present with others: our inner discomfort. You feel bad in relation to yourself, and so, on being with the other you are not alright. Your unease bothers you, making it difficult to give yourself to the present moment at the other's side. Instead of rejecting your apparently useless or harmful habits, be curious about finding out what is going on for you, by inquiring appreciatively into yourself. Looking is, in itself, akin to directing a spotlight on to the shadow, causing it to weaken until it fades away.

Rooting ourselves in our vital core

When we live out of our vital core, we open ourselves. Opening up helps us live in the present in such a way as to create the conditions for relationships to flourish. Well-rooted in our positive core, our inner healing strength, we open ourselves to other perspectives, helping us to see burdens from another angle and making the weight more relative. We feel lighter, we feel the energy of love entering and illuminating us, giving us confidence and hope. We can learn to be present and fully conscious without allowing the source of life that lives in us to be overshadowed by what the other is living through. Instead of making the other's problem our own, we can help them be freed from their burden by accompanying them, assisting them in connecting to their vital core. Sometimes a gesture is enough; at other times it is important to stay steady in an attitude of receptivity and listening. (See more on the positive core in the chapter: The vital core.)

Attitude of receptivity and listening

One of the ways to be present to the other is by listening to them. Sometimes you realise that instead of listening you are waiting to speak. You are planning what you are going to say in your mind. You even interrupt in order to put your own ideas forward. The person talking to you grasps that you are not really paying them attention, so they stop sharing what really matters to them with you. When they stop talking about it, not only do you not find out what is crucial for them, but they lose the chance to express and clarify it. Talking helps us to clarify our ideas. If we keep them internalised, we remain confused. By putting them into words, we air them and find greater clarity. So, to accompany the other in expressing themselves, we should be capable of silencing our mind and being receptive without interrupting with our own ideas.

When listening, it is very helpful to allow yourself and others silence; it isn't always necessary to answer immediately. You can reflect, be silent, perceive, grasp what is being said, tune in to your intuition and then answer. To really show you care, you should let the other finish saying everything they want, not invent possible answers in your mind. Leaving a space for silence allows you to give more meaningful answers.

Sometimes, rather than listening without saying anything, it is good to paraphrase or share what you feel in response to what you are hearing. That way the person talking to you can know what is happening in you while you are listening to them. It is good to express what you feel without adding either opinions or judgments. The most important thing at that moment is to be there, present, with the intention and practice of listening to what they are saying to you.

Being listened to is comforting in itself. Sometimes all someone needs is to be heard. Verbalising what they are thinking and feeling allows them to clarify what is happening inside themselves. In listening to them you support them in becoming aware of their next step. This is very powerful. By listening without intervening with advice you have allowed them to tune into their inner wisdom. This boosts their self-esteem and hope, making it easier to believe in themselves, that, yes, they can.

This kind of listening is not easy; it is not just sitting down and listening. You have to be centred in your healthy core and listen without judging. It isn't just an empathic kind of listening, but rather a generative one. What sometimes happens is that what the person says is not really what their being wants to express. By listening from a meditative state, you can read and understand between the words. Your listening is whole. Your "third ear" is alert and active. The third ear is the inner hearing of the self in the same way as we speak of the third eye as the eye of inner wisdom. When our listening is generative, we don't focus on the world of objects and facts; instead, we concentrate on listening to the story of a living being in evolution. Otto Scharmer[79] suggests generative listening, where: "I can't express what I experience in words. My whole being has slowed down. I feel more quiet and present and more my real self. I am connected to something larger than myself." This way of listening connects us to a deep space that seeks to break through. It means listening, from that place, to the future possibility that is being born. It is about accessing our ability to connect to the highest future possibility that might come about. We stop searching outside of ourselves: "… by the end of the conversation you are no longer the same person you were when it began. You have gone through a subtle but profound change that has connected you to a deeper source of knowing, including the knowledge of your best future possibility and self."

"We can only hear what is within if we open ourselves and are ready to meet what we find. When listening, it is not up to us to determine what we will find. We should be prepared to receive whatever comes as if we were an antenna."[80]

We often listen with filters, a self-defence mechanism so as not to attend to what we don't want to hear.

When I accompany someone, and they want to express something and make me a participant in their story, I try to put myself into a receptive attitude so that I can receive something of their experience. I try to perceive and grasp their message, so that I can be a mirror to them, reflecting their message back so they feel encouraged to express themselves in depth. It is a way of loving and taking care of them, of them feeling understood, accepted and loved. When offering my interlocutor the opportunity to express themselves, I don't want to judge, interpret, explore or reassure. I only wish to participate in their experience. My responses need to incorporate the experience that the other wants to communicate.

In reality, what a person wants to receive is not a ready-made solution, but rather to be accompanied and enabled in seeing clearly and finding a resolution. Hearing has consequences and, when accompanying people, I have experienced what Carl Rogers describes on many occasions:[81] "When I truly hear a person and the meanings that are important to him at that moment, hearing not simply his words, but him, and when I let him know that I have heard his own private personal meanings, many things happen. There is first of all a grateful look. He feels released. He wants to tell me more about his world. He surges forth in a new sense of freedom. He becomes more open to the process of change. I have often noticed that the more deeply I hear the meanings of this person, the more there is that happens."

To do this, for me it has been very important to learn not to interrupt someone who finds it difficult to express their feelings with my experiences. It often happens that the other person has feelings and attitudes that they find hard to explain or cannot yet express. They also have an emotional and spiritual depth that they struggle to communicate. They are only going to begin to let go if they feel assured of being received with intent and trust.

Being listened to generates deep satisfaction. Listening to each other mutually, with the sensitive skill to hear, communicate and open up to the other, helps us realise that the problem, in general, is not as big as it seemed. The other's perspective allows us to see things in context, especially when it protects us, accompanying us and giving us strength.

Are you present to the other?

When you are present with your thoughts and feelings of pain, you discover that you make contact with your potential of inner resources. They come out into the light. We have acquired habits that are more mindless (lacking attention, unaware) than mindful (connected to full attention); they are practices that disconnect us, distancing us from being fully present. It is common to reach for a cigarette or drink as a way of being less present. Going shopping when we don't need anything can be an automatic practice – *mindless*. It is not so much the action, but more the mental state it evokes that turns it into a *mindless* practice; that is, it disconnects us from the power of our presence. This state of distraction has a price. We lose a lot of our life. We lose the feeling of vitality and our ability to respond. We lose the ability to be present to the other.

When you are in a place that is taken up with a lot of activity and people, such as a central train station or a shopping centre, you watch people, and soon, you aren't present to yourself; rather, your mind wanders into the imaginary stories of the people who walk or run in front of you, going round and round. You begin to analyse, to judge – you like some of them, others you don't, you look from one place to another, following them. Within minutes, you are absorbed in endless scenes and you are no longer present. This also happens when we are with others in less crowded places. By being absorbed in our mind-stories, we are absent and closed to feeling the other.

When our mind is full of uncertainties, with opinions, judgments and fixed roles, we are not fully present. We cannot see what is in front of us and are conditioned by our own judgments and assumptions. Stop making assumptions, advises Thich Nhat Hanh, and you will avoid much unnecessary suffering. "We tend to make assumptions and above all to draw conclusions. The problem is that by doing this we believe what we suppose is true and create a reality around it. And it is not always positive or guided by trust or love, but more frequently by fear and our own insecurity."[82]

We will see more about being present to the other below.

111

Being present

If we focus on the quality of this instant with full awareness, we will live in a more whole way and be open to receiving and giving more. This is only possible if we are fully present. Opening ourselves to perception takes us to the present.

Perceiving

When you are present in mind and body at the same time, you are more aware of how you feel. You live experience directly and don't filter it through concepts or beliefs. You live what is and what you feel. What often happens is that "we have become disassociated from our hands, our skin, our eyes, our mouth, our nose, our heart. Feeling is the best aphrodisiac. First we should perceive it, then accept it, next, respect it and, finally, enjoy it."[83]

The path towards being present begins with perception. "To perceive means to become conscious. Perception is a spiritual matter, an activity of consciousness. The organs of the senses carry knowledge to consciousness. We can exercise perception beginning with the senses. Step by step, we will reach the most spiritual perceptions. Staying with perception means to also stay in the present. We can move to the past and the future through thoughts and desires. What exists in this moment is only the present. The past has gone. Only the memory of it and its results remain. The future is yet to come. Being realistic means to stay in the present. Being constantly attentive to the present will take us to the presence of God. Perception, consciousness, existence and remaining in the present are practically synonymous.

"Perception does not tire. Thinking and doing tire. Perception is the perfect form of rest. It revives and regenerates our strength. The one that truly rests enters slowly into contemplation. And the one who enters contemplation recovers their strength. All people perceive out of necessity, but after a fraction of a second our mind starts working. In this way we remove our attention from perception, taking it towards our ideas. We should learn to stay with perception."[84]

Do you spend more time in your thoughts than your senses? Your senses lead you to your perception and perceiving brings you to the present. When you realise that "you have gone" and are no longer present, it is easy to return to your body and your sensations. If you recognise how they are changing all the time, you can see that the feelings and thoughts you cling to are also impermanent and changing. Returning to your body and your sensorial perceptions roots you in the present moment. Meditating also brings you to this instant. In meditating you are present and you don't judge; you allow what is to be. You don't go round and round, over and again, about what is, trying to clarify this and that. **On allowing what breaks through in the moment to be, it becomes clearer, until you see, think and feel with clarity.**

Our presence for the other

Sometimes you want to help someone else in order to feel good yourself, not because you really want to help them. This might be what happens when you want another person to change or when you are trapped into proving something to yourself, justifying yourself. When this is the case, you cannot be present to the other. The teacher Thich Nhat Hanh advises: "Pay attention to the other's true situation, since if you don't, what you offer them may not be right for them."[85]

The essential thing when it comes to taking care of each other is to be present. We should learn to be with others without the interferences and interruptions that arise from trying to change them. It is about being present, free of prejudices, attachments and attempts to fix or control things. It is about accepting their reality as it is in the moment and being with them while they experience their feeling, accompanying them as they feel through their confusion and ask themselves what to do next. It seems simple, but the faster our mind gets distracted, the faster we disconnect and are not present. We forget again and again to be where we are, and we take ourselves somewhere else with our mind.

Without the ability to be present to the other, none of the techniques of psychotherapy, coaching or any other helping approach will move things on significantly. Without knowing how to be present with the other in their suffering, even if you are a therapist with many techniques, you won't really be able to contribute to the other person's advancement. It is with our whole presence that we can embrace the other and accompany them in their process.

Being present in uncertainty and discomfort

In general, our actions are based on our habitual behaviour, which we no longer question. Instead of choosing to be present and attentive at each moment, we stay trapped in the comfort of what is familiar. For example, sometimes you are kind to people because it is easier to be kind than to really be of help, to roll up your sleeves to get involved in caring for them, accompanying them in what they need or what they are going through.

When we see suffering, we want to eliminate it, but our desire to alleviate it gets mixed up with our desire to be comfortable and not upset by the other's pain. We have doubts about offering help and withdraw when we might have offered something valuable. Someone cries at work and we feel uncomfortable; we are not sure what to do and end up pretending that we aren't aware they are upset. At times we withdraw because we don't want the inconvenience or discomfort that getting involved might cause. We withdraw because we don't like how we feel when we don't know what to do to care for or give relief to someone else.

Being present in the uncertainty of what to do or not do allows us to be available to the other. The first step is a willingness to be present.

When we run from uncertainty and uncomfortable feelings,

we lose contact with the current experience, with what is happening to us here and now. Often it isn't what the other does or says that makes us uncomfortable, but rather what we feel when we are with them. Being prepared to help implies knowing how to live with uncertainty and our uncomfortable feelings.

At other times, it is not avoiding discomfort that motivates us but the opposite: we get too close. Then we are with someone else who is full of uncertainty, insecurity, worry and fear; we are present and we can feel what the other feels more fully. That can lead to becoming contaminated by their pain. If this happens, we may feel we want to change the focus of the conversation so that we can escape from the discomfort of feeling bad. If we are in a good place with ourselves, we will be able to tolerate those feelings without wanting to run away or change the conversation. We will be able to simply be there, alongside the uncertainty or pain that the other person is feeling.

When someone is with another person but their mind is on the past or future, on what they have to do next or what happened before, they are not present and the communication they establish is terrible, because they neither listen nor speak in a fully present way. The opportunity for a real encounter is lost, and it is just a routine meeting, ordinary, with nothing new or special in it. For this not to happen, be aware that your presence and the way you act have an influence. Believe in yourself. Remember that power lies in your presence in the now. Consider each encounter sacred, and increase your presence, be it with a friend, your partner, a client, a supplier, business colleague or your son or daughter. If you are with a client, be with them fully. If you are with your daughter, give yourself completely. Make each person you are with feel they are the most important thing for you at that moment. **Make each encounter into an unforgettable experience. Share the best of yourself.** Make the conversation meaningful and don't evade it with superfluous conversations and distracted looks. Let your presence and being bring difference, quality, care and clarity.

Be contagious by being yourself

The best care you can offer another begins by simply being you. What helps one person doesn't help someone else. Being present means being yourself and listening to what the other needs, adapting to the other's rhythm. It is about learning to be with the other without trying to control or change their process. By accepting their present reality, you accompany them while they feel what they feel; you feel their confusion and bring your presence, keeping your heart aware and your mind attentive. Your solid presence helps in the situation and you transmit the message that the other is basically good and capable, they can look for alternatives and things can be put right. You open up paths of hope.

Often, the best you can do is help the other person find their own resources. You simply have to be present, but often it is better not to offer your answers. It is much more valuable for the other to find their own answers. You reassure them by communicating that they are capable of recognising their own problems and solving them themselves. It is not just a question of telling them this with words, but communicating it to them in such a way that you are contagious and they can feel it.

For our presence to transmit positivity, vitality and clarity, we need to be aligned in body, emotion, mind and spirit. We should be centred and connected in such a way that we bring light with our presence. In that way, we can heal – "patch over" – broken, fractured or wounded hearts, and contribute towards healing wounds.

The presence of certain people in your life can make you forget pain. When a good friend looks you in the eyes and transports you to a space of tenderness and acceptance, your fears dissolve instantly. At that moment you stop blaming yourself and looking for guilty parties. The energy of loving consciousness has acted through the look and presence of the other.

Your healing presence

There is a healing presence, for example, when a doctor or a person who knows how to care takes your hand and transmits a healing energy to you that feeds your hope. They say words to you that act like a balm for your heart. There was alchemy in the contact and your pain seems to dissolve.

For your presence to be healing, you should transmit healthy vibrations, calming vibrations. Many people live in a state of ongoing suffering. The world needs consoling presences that offer help and alleviate the suffering of broken hearts, minds that are out of control, lives without meaning, spirits without direction.

To alleviate someone's suffering, have a generous heart. Often it is not necessary to give advice. Your supportive, collaborative presence helps and you give off calm and loving vibrations. You can practise this, even if you are not physically with the person who is suffering. Your vibrations travel through space and they arrive. Trust. Try not to suffer because the other person is suffering. A suffering heart will struggle to heal another suffering heart. It is the same as a doctor who gets ill and can no longer heal someone else who is sick; they themselves become a patient. Doctors protect themselves from contagion so that they are able to heal.

Sometimes the person can be emotionally, mentally, intellectually or spiritually malnourished. They seem to have a large void and are in need of sustenance, hungry to be nourished. A nourishing presence feeds your spirit, strengthening your wings and giving you room to fly; it feeds your mind by offering you positive content for reflection and feeds your heart with good feelings. Its presence is relaxing and in it your body lets go of tensions and your being recovers and feels embraced, recognised and appreciated. Surrounded by a presence that fully nourishes, your being fills up. It is like a vibration that soaks into your being and your body. As it fills you, it cleans you from other heavy energies. It renews you and cares for you. It is a presence that doesn't impose, it doesn't place obligations on you or restrict you.

When your presence is nourishing, you create a space for the organic development of others. You generate a space that is like the womb: a place that is secure and protected, where the foetus feels nourished and safe. The new being grows and develops in that space until it is ready to come out with all its resources to live and deal with the challenges of life.

A person with a presence that nourishes and sustains is connected to their inner resources and the resources that the Universe places at our disposal. They feel those resources to be within reach. They are also open to the Divine Presence. In channelling all these resources, people are led to a higher level in such a way that they transcend the I, me and mine; they leave their comfort zones and self-imposed limitations. When your presence is an upholding one, you inject energy and raise your personal vibration, lifting it up and bringing it close to the potential that lies dormant in everyone.

An example of a person whose presence nourished and sustained many others was Saint Teresa of Ávila. She worked with the Divine Presence, making room for it to act in her. Her life and her words speak to and inspire people of different nationalities, religions and cultures. Her presence has lasted throughout the centuries and transcends the limitations of any one particular belief system. It has nourished many pilgrims on the path and those seeking the divine essence.

To nourish and sustain, you have to embrace and welcome; thus will your presence calm agitated minds and "repair" broken hearts. You achieve this by sharing elevated thoughts that relax the mind, and pure feelings to heal and mend the pieces of the heart.

For your presence to be nourishing, you should feed your mind with positive thoughts. **Nourish your heart with good feelings.** Feed yourself with the perennial wisdom: read good books, have enriching conversations, participate in workshops that connect you to what is meaningful and help you to know yourself better. Tune in to your inner resources, your kindness and ability to love, hold dialogue and connect with the other. Embrace yourself so that you can embrace the other. Love yourself so that you can love the other.

Giving and giving from the self

"The human being does not find lasting happiness in getting something, but rather in giving oneself to something greater than themselves. Thus it is easier for them to separate from everything they have and free themselves of their attachments."[86] "Giving ourselves is our truest joy and it is a liberation because through giving of self we are joined with the infinite."[87]

Happiness isn't about acquiring things, competences or privileges that make the "I" bigger, but rather comes through surrender and self-giving. According to the Buddhist perspective, the separate and individualised I is more a problem than a solution when seeking to reach wholeness. What arises from the separated I is the ego, an ego that is hungry to possess.

If we observe nature, we see that she is generous. The sun gives light, heat, life; the trees give fruit, oxygen, shade; and water gives life, cleaning and regenerating: we might say that nature lives in abundance and regeneration. As human beings, we might identify this virtue of nature in altruistic attitudes and the value of generosity. When you give yourself, you open yourself, you grow, mature and the best version of you reveals itself. When you are authentic, you stimulate the authenticity of others, and thus the freedom to give and receive love is greater.

Some people find it hard to give of themselves, not because their priority is to look after themselves, but rather because they are overwhelmed by the fear of being hurt, of reviving a wound, or afraid that they won't know how to and don't want to open up. There are people who are always needy; yet, were they to give themselves and care for others, their permanent dissatisfaction would disappear. A double movement takes place when we care and help, both outwards and inwards; we connect to others and to ourselves. When you love and are loving towards others and in what you do, you feel whole. Your wholeness lies in giving and giving of yourself. On doing so, you are revitalised, and exhaustion, despair, lack of hope and apathy disappear. When you love, centred in your vital core and out of your free being, open, transparent and available, you feel whole and flow with what life presents you; you give and receive. You connect to altruism.

Being altruistic leads you to expand beyond your private world and your personal preferences to share with others. Feeling that we all form part of the same world makes our hearts bigger, makes us more tolerant, loving and compassionate. On being in relationship, we feel that our pain is theirs, we are not isolated, and the other's pain is ours. Their joy is also ours, and our achievements and joys are theirs. We share. "The altruist seeks the realisation of the *we*. The limits of the I are transcended. Altruism is only possible through the extension of the I and not through its destruction."[88]

Giving and giving from the self is a bidirectional movement which is also about opening oneself to the other's love, accepting their way of loving you. Some give too much, forgetting themselves, and end up exhausted. They turn others into their priority and stop taking care of themselves. You may give a lot to the other, but not allow the other to give themselves to you. You expect them to love you or attend to you in a specific way, and when they don't, you close yourself to their way of sharing with you. I am not only referring to the relationship between couples, but also to relationships of friendship, work, of business partners and colleagues.

I was working for a time on a project that I gave myself to completely. Our coexistence was very intense. We shared home, food and work on the project from early in the day till night. People from different places and backgrounds collaborated. Some came from very poor families; there were even the children of illiterate parents. I learned there that people loved me as they could and knew how, not as I expected them to. Realising this opened me, it relaxed me, and my expectations of emotional return lowered. Accepting the way that each person gave of themselves, from where he or she was, allowed for a more sincere and joyful coexistence and collaboration. Opening myself to how the other was able to give of themselves, and the extent that they could do so, allowed everyone to feel good about being themselves.

When you receive, you allow the other to give of themselves and thus express their beauty and feel their wholeness. Open yourself and learn to receive. It is about staying available while knowing how to place limits and be clear about what you need, what suits you, what you can offer and when. It is important to be specific about your availability and what you offer. It is better to offer something that is specific rather than very open-ended, such as: "Tell me if you need something." It is also important to dare to ask clearly. Offer and offer from yourself without renouncing your being. Make clear agreements and commitments. Sometimes our request is so ambiguous that the other doesn't understand it, and then you say to them: "But I told you clearly." Perhaps it was clear in your mind, but you didn't formulate it clearly. It is good to check that the other has understood what you have asked for or what you have offered. It is about being assertive, knowing how to ask and say yes or no when appropriate. It is also about giving yourself permission.

When being with the other, or others, leads us to lose our inner peace, we sometimes opt for narcissistic solitude. This means fewer possibilities to develop inner qualities and powers that are necessary to our coexistence, such as cooperation, asking, offering and agreeing, dialogue, active listening, empathy, loving and allowing oneself to be loved. We have fewer opportunities to face things, let go, be patient, forgiving and much more. We become possessive. On feeling possessive of the other, we deprive them of freedom, and deprive ourselves of our own. Then our requests turn into impositions. The other feels an obligation and is even almost afraid of not complying with your request. Let's learn to give ourselves out of freedom, happiness, joy and responsibility, not out of fear and obligation.

We can go a step further in our giving and ability to experience surrender. Let's see below.

Giving in and surrendering

When a man loves, giving becomes a matter of joy to him, like the tree's surrender of the ripe fruit.
Rabindranath Tagore[89]

Surrender is opening and freedom. In surrender you give in, letting go of resistance and opening yourself. To give in is to accept what you have and what you are on an inner level. It is to be open to life. The opposite is to put up resistance. To resist is to shrink within, it is a hardening of the ego, it is to close oneself. You surround yourself with armour to defend yourself. You do so because you are trying to protect yourself, but in doing it you hide yourself, cover your own shadows and flee from those of others. As Eckhart Tolle reminds us: "Non-resistance is the key to the greatest power in the Universe."[90] A new dimension of awareness opens up when you give in, when you surrender. The awareness with which you connect to that state of opening allows you to act in harmony with the whole. You feel supported by the creative intelligence. In that state, coincidences happen, people and circumstances help and accompany you in your next phase. If action is not possible, you stay with the inner calm that accompanies this state of surrender, handing over and acceptance.

Surrender and opening do not mean that limits are not placed. Sometimes people understand opening as being hospitable, and being hospitable as allowing people to come in and out of their space as it suits the other.

We can overwhelm the other with our generosity. An exaggerated generosity is sometimes accompanied by a lack of self-esteem and little respect towards oneself and one's own spaces. What manifests then is that love is understood as a total surrender whereby one allows the other to walk all over them and take advantage of them. That is not a healthy giving, given that one loses oneself. If you don't place limits and offer too much of yourself, you lose contact with your vital core and exhaust yourself; you ignore your needs and end up being more of a burden than a help.

Find out where you want to put your limits and make it known to the people you relate to. This can become problematic when you feel that you are being selfish by placing limits. Examine the beliefs you have around this difficulty and the stories you tell yourself in relation to the limits that you find hard to define. You can find clarity through writing, speaking to a good friend or quiet reflection. When you have done everything you can, it is good to recognise it and not ask more of yourself. Then it is time to let go and allow the other to evolve at their own pace, with their own resources.

Seeing the other

John, who has worked at a bank for forty years, shared his experience with me concerning a change of attitude that led him to great personal growth and increased his motivation for going to work. He feels that each encounter with "the client" is in fact an opportunity for a truly sacred encounter. So he sees his desk as an altar and every time he receives someone he turns that encounter into a true re-union. It may be the only time he will meet that person. At that moment, the most important thing for John is to be present to the person in front of him. Thus, the person, the client, takes away something more than a financial solution. They leave with the human warmth and freshness of a different kind of encounter.

A few minutes of kind and available presence, in which you see and recognise the other, can change people's direction and destiny. Robert is a lawyer and he told me how a few minutes of his presence helped a client and changed his destiny:

The court case was due within an hour and my client – assigned by state legal aid and who I didn't know – was in the cells in the old, dirty basement of the court buildings in Barcelona. The week before I had read and studied his case, and I was interested in talking to my client before the court appearance. The normal thing is that before the spoken hearing the judge gives you five minutes to talk to the accused. I don't feel comfortable with that, since you are obliged to talk to the accused in a very small space, in front of everybody, and your conversation is listened to by the others. That's why I asked the judge to give me a pass so that I could go to the cells. After some bureaucratic problems and a lot of persistence, with the pass in my hand, I went to the cells. There, the police officers – who were in charge – treated me like an intruder who was only going to cause trouble. "Only five minutes!" they warned me. I went down the narrow passageway flanked by the shared cells where the prisoners are held in groups of six or seven. They are like caves where you can't see anything from the passage. I shouted the name of my client. Out of the darkness and the shouts of the prisoners a young man appeared. "Hello," I said to him, "we only have five minutes: three for you to explain what really happened and two for me to tell you what you have to declare." He made his statement very well and in the end he was absolved. After a few weeks he came to my office and I congratulated him on his statement: clear and unhesitant. He answered me that my visit had given him the necessary strength; that he was the only prisoner visited by his lawyer before the case. That day I thought that he had really noticed my presence, my genuine interest in his problem, my confidence in him giving a good statement and my conviction that in the end his serious problem would be solved. Someone that he didn't know had been concerned about him.

Robert is highlighting a very important matter here, one that is at the root of our presence: seeing the other and recognising them, taking them out of their invisibility and making them visible at each encounter.

Appreciating and being appreciated

When we appreciate, we move forward: we discover the best of "what is" and open ourselves to glimpsing "what could be". Appreciating with a passionate and engrossing effort, investing emotional and cognitive energy, helps us generate a positive image of the future that we wish for. When we appreciate, new values arise.

In his book, David Cooperrider quotes the artist Vincent van Gogh in a letter to his brother, expressing what could be considered a complete course on the relationship between appreciation and the arising of new values:

I should like to paint a portrait of an artist friend, a man who dreams great dreams, who works as the nightingale sings, because it is in his nature; he'll be a fine man. I want to put into my picture of appreciation, the love I have for him. So I paint him as he is, as faithfully as I can. But the picture is not finished yet. To finish it, I am now the arbitrary colorist. I exaggerate the fairness of the hair, I come even to use orange tones, chromes and pale lemon-yellow. Behind the head, instead of painting the ordinary wall of a mean room, I paint infinity, a plain background of the richest, intensest blue that I can contrive – and by this simple combination of the bright head against the rich blue background, I get [a] mysterious effect, like a star in the depths of an azure sky.

Cooperrider continues:

Like Churchill, van Gogh began with a stance of appreciative cognition. He viewed his friend through a loving and caring, and focused on those qualities that "excited his preference" and kindled his imagination. The key point [says David Cooperrider] is that van Gogh did not merely articulate admiration for his friend: He created new values and new ways of seeing the world through the very act of valuing. And again, as Nietzsche has elaborated: "valuing is creating; hear it, ye creating ones! Valuation is itself the treasure and jewel of valuating things."[91]

The capacity to appreciate is born out of a mental state and attitude that manifests through the ability to perceive what is valuable and meaningful about oneself, the other, and the world and its circumstances. An appreciative attitude increases people's generative and influencing ability, and with it their skill to create healthy change is multiplied. Developing appreciative skills helps us create and increase our happiness and well-being. "Happiness is a mental state, a way of perceiving each other and perceiving ourselves and the world that surrounds us," says Sonja Lyubomirsky.[92]

When we appreciate ourselves, our self-esteem is

strengthened. On discovering and valuing the best of what we have, we provide ourselves with resources to deal with life. When this discovery is genuine, we feel an emotional connection to our strengths and abilities. Positive emotions awaken in us, such as self-respect, happiness, hope and inspiration, amongst others. We open ourselves to learning. If we have self-confidence, we dare to take risks. When we appreciate that what we do is important and can make a difference in our lives and the world, we feel strengthened and do whatever we are doing better.

When appreciating the other becomes a lifelong habit, we increase the quality of our relationships and help bring out the best in people. Unfortunately, we come across many people whose lives get stuck in complaining, focusing on what isn't going well, what isn't working, what they don't like. This makes it difficult to open oneself to appreciating. It can also happen that, on not being accustomed to living in appreciative environments, when we find someone who appreciates, mistrust arises and we ask ourselves: "Perhaps they want something from me? What is wrong with them? What are they looking for in me or from me?" Then, to protect ourselves, we react by trying to distance ourselves, creating an estrangement, a distant and impersonal position. We don't want to suffer and put up defences, or else we are afraid of becoming trapped and not knowing how to get out of an emotionally uncomfortable situation.

Can I allow myself to experience positive attitudes towards the other person, attitudes of quality, care, pleasing, interest, respect and appreciation? For a long time, I had a certain fear in the face of those feelings. I was afraid that if I allowed myself such feelings towards other people, I would find myself trapped by them. They might place demands on me, or I might disappoint them, and I didn't want to take those risks. With the practice of Appreciative Inquiry, having created the habit and attitude of appreciating, I have come to the conclusion that feeling and relating to the other as a person we experience positive feelings towards is not at all prejudicial. It brings us closer, opening us and bringing the best out of everyone.

However, on several occasions, and to my surprise, my expression of appreciation towards men has made them think and feel that I was nurturing feelings for them. Sometimes they receive such little appreciation that when I share it, they find it hard to receive because they think I am in love with them, something they are afraid of or resist. Then they keep a distance. They close themselves to receiving feelings of appreciation. Even so, I have discovered the great value of appreciating, and I continue to do so. When we are not afraid of giving and receiving positive feelings, it is easier to appreciate people.

I have learned that it is not dangerous to give or receive tender and positive feelings. This helps me get close to people, and I have become more open to this closeness. A few years ago, I kept my distance. Now it is easier to get closer to me, and easier for me to get closer to others.

"One of the most satisfying feelings I know – and also one of the most growth-promoting experiences for the other person – comes from my appreciating this individual in the same way that I appreciate a sunset. People are just as wonderful as sunsets if I can let them *be*. In fact, perhaps the reason we can truly appreciate a sunset is that we cannot control it […] I don't *try* to control a sunset. I watch it with awe as it unfolds. I like myself best when I can appreciate my staff member, my son, my daughter, my grandchildren, in this same way. I believe this is a somewhat Oriental attitude; for me it is a most satisfying one. […] When I am prized, I blossom and expand, I am an interesting individual. In a hostile or unappreciative group, I am just not much of anything. […] I wish I had the strength to be more similar in both kinds of groups."[93]

Perhaps it is the same for you as for many others: easier to appreciate than to receive appreciation. I identify with Rogers' experience:

> I feel warmed and fulfilled when I can let in the fact, or permit myself to feel, that someone cares for, accepts, admires, or prizes me. Because of elements in my past history, I suppose, it has been very difficult for me to do this. For a long time I tended almost automatically to brush aside any positive feelings aimed in my direction. My reaction was: "Who, me? You couldn't possibly care for me. You might like what I have done, or my achievements, but not me." This is one respect in which my own therapy helped me very much. I am not always able even now to let in such warm and loving feelings from others, but I find it very releasing when I can do. I know that some people flatter me in order to gain something for themselves; some people praise me because they are afraid to be hostile. But I have come to recognise the fact that some people genuinely appreciate me, like me, love me, and I want to sense that fact and let it in. [...] Like many others, I used to fear being trapped by letting my feelings show.[94]

Appreciate and open yourself to receiving appreciation; beauty and vital energy will flow in your life, you will be stronger, and your potential will flourish.

Accepting

One of the great advances on the path towards the care of oneself and the other takes place when you accept *what is* and you accept by allowing *what is* to be.

What Is, Is

Accepting reality, accepting the other and yourself, means not manipulating situations so that they fit into your ideas of how they ought to be. Accepting means that you don't judge your experience. You do not have to like or dislike what happens inside you. Leave it be. **What is, is.** Don't start constructing stories about it, labelling it as negative or positive. Don't keep thinking about it. It is about knowing how to be with what you feel and how to live with it. Accepting emotions, such as anger, jealousy, envy, sadness and fear, allows you to recognise them. Once you manage to accept them, you will be able to separate yourself from them, connecting to tenderness and kindness towards yourself. Try to be gentle with yourself instead of self-censoring and being harsh on yourself for how you feel.

It may be that your feelings are "petty emotions", such as impatience due to the slowness of the supermarket cashier, or jealousy when someone recognises another person and seems not to see you, or irritation because your husband or wife doesn't intuit what you want. Or you may have "big feelings", such as sadness and grief over the loss of a loved one, the fear of death, the uncertainty of not knowing what to do to help someone in need, or the weight you feel when there is a typhoon in China, or a hurricane or earthquake in Central America or somewhere else. All these feelings constitute part of what connects us to each other. On feeling sadness, you can understand someone who is sad better. You realise that many other people share these feelings. Your experiences make you more human, more understanding towards yourself and others.

Accepting does not mean we agree with what is happening, nor that we let something that causes harm escape punishment. For example, I can accept that I have made a mistake, that I have failed, but rather than berating myself, recognising it with an attitude of warmth allows me to stay connected to my healthy core and hold my head high, instead of hanging my head in shame. Perhaps I did what I did that caused harm because I wasn't connected to my positive core or in a state of full awareness.

The ideal is to develop an attitude of acceptance rather than judgment in all aspects of your experience. This gives you inner peace and allows you to see without getting attached, or anxious. This acceptance is necessary to reach a state of equanimity, one of the basic pillars in Buddhism for living a whole life and dissolving suffering.

Accepting allows for the encounter with the other

The encounter is the most beautiful possibility between two people. An encounter takes place out of the acceptance and conserving of the shared mysteries. Being able to accept another person as they are relaxes you and brings you pleasure. The acceptance of what is different is one of the essential steps in the experience of love.

When I accept a person with the feelings, attitudes and beliefs they manifest as a real and vital part of themselves, I am helping them become a person who is connected to themselves. To build bridges from your being and experience towards other people, it is good to allow yourself to be yourself, and the other to be him or herself. On accepting them, I also accept their right to use their experience in their own way and find their own meanings in it.

Conditioned by our beliefs, life habits, culture and other aspects, questions arise: "Do I accept each one of the aspects that the other person presents me with? Can I accept them as they are? Can I communicate this attitude to them? Or, do I only receive them conditionally, accepting some aspects of their feelings and rejecting others openly or in a disguised form?"

When my attitude is conditional, the other person finds it harder to change and perhaps cannot develop in the aspects that I can't accept. When, later, I discover the reasons that prevented me from accepting aspects of them, I realise the other person was acting as a mirror, showing me their feelings, which I shared and didn't want to see in myself. If my intention is to offer better help, first I need to develop and accept those aspects in myself.

Accepting gives security

When people feel threatened from the outside, they are consumed by defending themselves, making it difficult for them to take care of the inner feelings and the conflicts that represent sources of threats.

One threat might be external evaluation. In almost all the phases of our life – at home, school, work – we are subject to rewards and punishments imposed by outside judgments. Value judgments do not foster personal development. "... a positive evaluation is as threatening in the long run as a negative one, since to inform someone that he is good implies that you also have the right to tell him that he is bad. So I have come to feel that the more I can keep a relationship free of judgment and evaluation, the more this will permit the other person to reach the point where he recognizes that the locus of evaluation, the centre of responsibility, lies within himself. The meaning and value of his experience is in the last analysis something which is up to him, and no amount of external judgment can alter this. So I should like to work toward a relationship in which I am not, even in my own feelings, evaluating him. This I believe can set him free to be a self-responsible person."[95]

Sometimes, as a friend, the only thing I can do is listen. I realise that the mere fact of sharing the difficulty can lighten the load of the person talking to me. If that person identifies their problem, naming it and listening to it while we look it in the face, we humanise it. What happens at times is that the shame or fear of what others will think when they see our vulnerabilities or weaknesses, or of being labelled as failures, makes it difficult for us to share our suffering. Under the appreciative look and constructive conversation, that fear dissipates. When I explicitly recognise the value of the person opening up, I create a space of trust so that they can dare to express themselves.

It would be great if we learned to accompany suffering

without judging the other. A loving gaze that receives our pain, not judging when we open ourselves to being heard and sharing, helps us express ourselves and let go of the suffering accumulated inside us. Although we might think we will be judged or seen in a bad light, we discover the look of tenderness and understanding of the other who draws close to us, and that is deeply liberating. The weight of the burden that can fall on someone can be lightened if they have somewhere to express and show it. Being seen humanises us and allows us to move on. We can broaden how we look at someone, accepting them, opening to them and silencing the voice that labels and judges.

When I feel free to be myself, neither depending on external evaluations nor fearing them, I discover that I can understand and accept the other person in greater depth, because I am not afraid of losing myself. When I cling to another's evaluation of me, I leave my core and fall into trying to please or be according to the other.

Accepting the past and reconciling experiences

You can resist returning to yourself, given that, as Thich Nhat Hahn states: "Most people are afraid of returning to themselves because they fear facing the pain that is inside them."[96]

Sometimes we find it hard to accept situations we have lived through. They caused us suffering that we consider unacceptable. Coming to fully accept our past helps us be at peace with ourselves and others. To achieve this, you might have to ask for forgiveness or to forgive, or clear things up in one way or another; or perhaps it means doing the work of transforming a negative experience into a learning one. Whatever it takes, it is worth trying. If you don't fully accept the past, you won't be comfortable in the present and you may become frustrated, depressed, have a breakdown or simply be in a bad mood with unstable emotional states that are difficult to control. Every time a present situation evokes that painful past, the wound will open and continue to bleed. Accepting the past is to allow the wound to close and means that, although it is still there, it no longer hurts or overwhelms us internally.

Accepting what has happened can mean accepting loss, or that you were taken in, accepting your mistake and/or that of the other, accepting that they hurt you or accepting that someone killed a loved one or they died in an accident. The neurologist Maria Gudin says that getting over wrongs is an extremely important task, because hate and revenge poison our lives. **Forgiving oneself and others opens the channels to heal the damaged heart.**

To achieve this we need to recover control over our mind and thoughts. Some people believe that forgiving is an act of weakness. On the contrary, forgiving shows that we are in charge of our well-being and no longer victims of the other. Forgiving allows us to recover our inner power. Without that control, our mind will go to that place of suffering over and over again; it will repeat the "Why me? How dare they?" loop. The thoughts will be like a constant hammering, making it hard to control the feelings of anger, frustration and sadness. Like woodworm, your own thoughts will make holes in the root of your being and you will end up exhausted, without energy. At that moment you will have forgotten the first principle of leadership: nobody creates your thoughts or feelings except you, yourself.

Bill Clinton telephoned Nelson Mandela two hours after he came out of prison, after many years' imprisonment for fighting for human rights, and he asked him how he could so easily forgive those who had jailed him. Mandela answered that if he were to hate them, they would continue to control him. If we don't forgive, we stay tied to the people who have upset us. We lose freedom, which blocks our creativity and feeds our frustration. This causes violence in us. There is a lot of rage and violence in the world, and this energy destroys us. We won't create a better world out of rage.

When Ela Gandhi was asked what she had learned from her grandfather, she said, amongst many other things: "If you want to overcome your enemy, love him." In that love there is compassion. In compassion there is forgiveness. Don't bear grudges. In accepting you stay open. You put the clock back to zero, that is, you let go of prejudices, images from the past and feelings of blame.

Richard, Janet's son, falsified documents to take her properties from her. Janet was deceived, robbed and lied to by her son. Her pain was huge. Her trust in Richard was broken and the relationship deteriorated so much that it became a non-relationship. Janet meditated, forgave and was able to accept; this allowed her to remake her life. At the same time, she went to court and followed the legal steps to find solutions. But the meditation, forgiveness and acceptance were what made it possible for her to go on living in peace.

Janet's story is a tough example of how relationships can become a source of deep pain. If the person remains steeped in pain, anger, sadness and fear, their life ends up being hell. **Accepting what is and forgiving allows us to move on.** If I am diagnosed with cancer and I remain absorbed by grief, anger and fear, those emotional states will make things even worse for me.

Accepting does not mean being in agreement. Accepting means the possibility of getting your personal power back in order to face and live through what you have to from your centre of personal power; that is, your healthy core.

Sometimes you need to reconcile yourself with your past and transform the fears that your experiences might trigger. For example, you are driving a car and have an accident. Then it takes you some time to drive again, because the memory of the accident awakens the fear of having another or reliving the one you already had. Someone who has never had an accident gets into the car confidently, because they don't have this scene imprinted in their mind, not having experienced it.

The fears we carry inside us are not of the present. Something happened to us in the dark, and we are afraid of the dark. Fears in relationships: you opened your heart, you fell in love and, over time, you got hurt. You got wounded here, you got wounded there and you felt hurt, misunderstood, manipulated, deceived or mistreated. So now you don't open your heart for anything; it is "protected", enclosed by the armour that you yourself created. You live on the defensive and, if you open yourself, you do so very cautiously.

If you wish to go beyond defensive attitudes and fears that are rooted in the experiences you have had, you have to reconcile yourself with your past, fully accepting it and knowing how to protect yourself healthily, living open instead of closed. You cannot change your past. What you can change is how you fit your past into the present. Bemoaning and complaining about the past does not help you.

You may need to heal your experience of the past. As in Janet's example, we see that part of the past is healed through forgiveness. Without forgiving, you can't forget. Forgiving helps us start a new chapter: what was is over now. It no longer is. It no longer is, except in your own mind. Practise the motto: "What has happened is already the past." You don't need to think about it so often. Don't allow your mind to relive it. Value your time. Value its creation: thoughts. We need to realise that when we project on to others and blame them for our rage, we allow ourselves to be their slaves and victims. Clinging on is harmful. Acceptance liberates us. To reach it, we require mental power that allows us to stop the repetitive thoughts causing unhappiness. You can strengthen your mind through affirmations. Louise Hay suggests this one: "I forgive you for not being the way I wanted you to be. I forgive you and I set you free."

The work to see which aspects of your past are weighing you down and to clear up your own past requires silence, reflection and meditation. When you reconcile yourself with your own past, you can free yourself of the burden that it meant. You reach a point of not being afraid that the past might come back to you. Because, if not, at times it is like a shadow pursuing you. If you were robbed, you are followed by the shadow that you might be robbed again; if hurt, you fear it might happen again. Whatever happens, that experience presents itself in dreams sometimes, in the subconscious or in present attitudes. Reliving the past in your mind, you don't fully enjoy the present. If it was a traumatic experience, it is good to receive help with healing it, to be able to move on in a more agile and efficient way.

It is good to put the pieces of your past together so that they don't carry on generating upsets or act as obstacles that stop you living fully. You can fit them together, accept that you had to live through them and live the present with a constructive vision of the future. Going over and over what you went through, asking yourself, "Why me? How was it possible?", will only irritate the wound and delay its healing.

During a period of my life it helped me to write letters to God about my experiences. The exercise of sharing them with God in writing gave me clarity and helped me to bring the divine light to my life in order not to be loaded down with experiences, unhappiness or unnecessary burdens. Have you ever written to God? You can also write without addressing the letter to anybody. Simply write and let what is inside come out. I used to do it at night, telling God about the things that affected me or that I had learned. I told Him intimate things or feelings that other people perhaps wouldn't understand or wouldn't be there to listen to. I also used to tell Him everything that I was asking myself questions about. The following morning, early, when I meditated and studied, I often used to receive answers, and saw things with greater clarity. It is about writing and letting go of what you feel, handing it over to "something, or someone" beyond you, be that the Whole, the universe, life or God.

Welcoming

When we are open and appreciate all the people who appear in our life, we welcome them in, we learn, we love and we grow together. This opening is made easier by an attitude of learning and moving forward.

"It is not easy to describe the immense good that one can do when they put themselves in a welcoming attitude of receiving, with huge respect, what the other wants to transmit to them. The people around you realise very quickly, they feel trust and begin to open themselves. They feel themselves to be a liberated person. They learn to know themselves. In a word, they begin to live."[97]

When we invite someone home, we prepare the dwelling so that it is welcoming: we clean, we put out flowers, making it nice and getting rid of the rubbish. In the same way, to be with the other in full opening, it is good to clean out our inner storage cupboards and our minds, clarifying our intentions, releasing prejudices, cultivating acceptance and getting ourselves into a welcoming attitude.

When opening ourselves and being available to the other, we don't know what we are inviting in nor what will appear. Being open and present to the other requires full trust in our resources to experience what might arise. Being present to others can be full of challenges. In intimate connection to the other, we can come to feel their pain so deeply that we make it our own. Experiencing their anguish and confusion can make it difficult for us to stay open and present.

When you have a family member, a loved one or a friend who is suffering, you can receive their suffering, but if you want to help them get free of it, focus on their desire for growth and their longings. You can ask them a question that accompanies them in seeing their light, that changes the direction they are looking in, and their thinking. Instead of focusing on the shadow, let them look at the light, their vital core, what moves them to live, what makes them whole, and that way they can come to be grateful for what they are and what they have.

It is about recognising the suffering and pain that the other feels while also understanding their desire for growth and development, and focusing on the latter. We don't have to deny the appearance of suffering or the expression of vulnerability. It is not about digging deeper into the causes of the suffering, wallowing in the whys and wherefores, or taking the other to even greater depths of their affliction, but rather allowing them to observe themselves and change their outlook, change the angle they are positioning themselves from, to see and incorporate other perspectives. It is about seeing what the suffering makes possible and being aware of what it offers ("What is it telling you?"). It is a question of helping them get their inner power back so as not to remain emotionally devastated and mentally anguished. Going through the shadow, we dissolve it and reach the light. If you can't do it on your own, place yourself at the centre of your being where the source of the heathy core lies, and put the dark parts in front of it, handing it over to the power of the unconditional love of God, of the Whole. Contemplate the healthy core, or the presence of God, and don't get trapped by the dark. Recognise it and let it go. Perhaps you need to forgive in order to let go. Sometimes, not being able to love the people who make us suffer is more painful than the wound.

If you forgive and place your forgiveness before God you will feel redeemed. It isn't necessary to look for causes, but rather, it is a matter of receiving your suffering, or, in the words of Jalics, of suffering through it and handing it over to God. Then you will be redeemed and your affliction will not return. **So much light, strength and energy will come from the healthy core that you will find the courage to move forward.**

We can accompany each other, helping those at our side listen to themselves, to become aware that if they don't listen to what the suffering is signalling to them, a time will come when an inner chasm opens up. We flee from our own inner voices that want to communicate something to us. Receiving the suffering, making it ours, we will feel that it is speaking to us. The suffering is pointing to the possibility of a latent change, a transformation that can come about in greater depth. **When we find the meaning of our suffering, it is transformed.**

When something motivates us, we face the difficulties that are presented in order to achieve it. Motivation pushes us forward. We can motivate ourselves by looking at images of the future that attract us, awakening motivation and enthusiasm in us. If we are motivated, it is easier to face suffering and be able to overcome it, making the transition through it with an appreciative gaze and a grateful perspective.

6. Taking Care of the Whole

When doing something I am linked with the whole world.
Within myself the world comes to itself, and in the world I come
alive. Action in which I lose myself is devotion. That is only possible
so long as I am not forced away in my thoughts from what is here
and now, backward into the past or forward into the future.[98]
Peter Schellenbaum

In this part, I present some ideas and suggestions to bear in mind when taking care of ourselves beyond the I and you, the place where we all meet.

Make peace with time: do less and achieve more

To take care of yourself means to keep periods of time free of obligations, leaving them available for yourself. It means dedicating a space to yourself, to be alone, quiet, in silence or with inspiring music. Not always being in a hurry. Having space and time to enjoy sacred spaces of creative emptiness; calming down, listening to and feeling oneself; eating in peace, eating well and healthily; not be constantly doing; tidying up and cleaning; to be perceiving and breathing consciously; stretching and flexing our muscles. It means knowing how to *be* without doing anything. Something new can arise out of the nothing, an inspiration or a refreshing thought. It is a space that allows us to see a relationship we hadn't seen or become aware of how we are and what is going on for us.

We also need to give ourselves permission to not always be hyper-responsible, with our schedules weighed down with obligations. To know how to let go of the "have to do" lists and be able to enjoy the landscape, the streets, the birds, looking around us and living in the moment. It is about walking without using the walk to make a phone call. To walk, walking. When

I walk, I walk. When I speak on the phone, I give it my full attention, as if the person on the other end of the line was in front of me. When I shower, I shower. Perhaps you are worrying about what you are going to do next when showering, and you slip. You weren't present to what you were doing. When you are eating, eat: savour the food and enjoy it. When we eat, our brain helps our digestion; if we occupy it by looking at emails, our mobile or reading, that is, with a mental and intellectual task, then it has to diversify its functions and the digestive process slows down.

Doing several things at the same time (multitasking) is less effective and slower than focusing on one task at a time.

How do you live in the moment? Are you so worried about the future that you live the present purely as a means of getting there? In this instant you can feel the anguish of what has happened to you, what happened, what you experienced, what was done to you and what you allowed to be done. In this moment you can feel the anxiety about what is to come but has not yet happened, about what you sense and feel nervous about, because you don't know what's going to happen, or when or how. You get through this moment torn between anguish and anxiety.

Instead of being anxious about time, focusing on the task at hand helps us enjoy the moment, to be more concentrated on what we are doing and, therefore, to do it better. Being clear about what takes priority in the moment and focusing on it helps us achieve more and struggle less. It is also good to learn to simplify. Many tasks are carried out more efficiently when made simpler. For example, you are stressed because you have many tasks left to do. To simplify, make yourself a list of tasks and matters that have to be dealt with. Look at the list and see what needs to be prioritised. Remake the list according to priority and get down to it with determination and clarity. After two weeks, there might be five things at the end of the list that haven't been done, and nothing terrible has happened. You were getting stressed for no good reason, overwhelmed by everything you had to do even without any outside pressure, but you freed yourself from the stress by focusing on priorities.

In general, we have tight schedules. Part of taking care of ourselves lies in knowing how to live our time well. It is beneficial for peace of mind and bodily relaxation to leave spaces empty in your schedule; times for the unforeseen to arise. If, in the end, nothing unforeseen comes up, you will have a period of time and space to breathe consciously and relax, call a friend or just enjoy doing nothing. If something unforeseen does arise, you won't have to rush or get stressed, you will have time for it. Also, save yourself a few more minutes so that you go to meetings in a more tranquil state, and when you go to catch planes or trains. What can in appearance seem like a waste of time saves us the stress of worrying about not arriving on time, having to explain why we arrived late, and having to run to get there. If you arrive early and have to wait, you are better able to prepare your contribution. The wait is not a waste of time; rather, it is time that you gain for yourself.

Allow yourself to enjoy waiting and feel the gift of those extra minutes when you can relax, be at peace, have a cup of tea or walk and move about. Knowing how to leave the mind in peace, being grateful for the gift of a moment of not having to rush, lets you ask yourself: "What is there here? What gift lies hidden behind this empty time or space?" When we have free time, the space that appears is pregnant with infinite possibilities waiting to be born and grow.

If I meet someone I know in the street or in a café and have enough time, it is a pleasure, since I can let myself have a conversation. In contrast, how sad when there is no spare time for the encounter, only enough for a hello and goodbye. This happens to Maggie, because she always arrives late to meetings, and is stressed on arriving. Then she has to set to explaining her delays. In filling her time up to the last minute, she ends up worn out, tired and looking rude. She does more and achieves less. I suggest turning this formula around and doing less to achieve more. Another example might relate to the order and cleanliness of children's bedrooms. How much time and energy do parents put in to achieve this? The mother, or father, gets angry, turns strict, annoyed, telling their child to tidy their room again and again. But it achieves little, and she ends up doing it, or the father or the cleaner. Perhaps if one acts as an unattached observer, allowing the child to live with their untidiness and dirtiness, a time will come when they see that if they don't take responsibility for it nobody else will. You, as a mother or father, do less and bring about, after a period of patience, the chance for your child to wake up and become responsible.

To make peace with time is to make peace with yourself. It is not about managing time. **Time is always full of abundance and potential.** The clock ticks – it doesn't ask us to manage it. What we need to manage are our minds and our actions. Let's be present to what we do and think. If you are brushing your teeth, brush them consciously, not thinking about other things. If you are walking, do it being present, with attention. That way, you won't trip, the walk will revitalise you, and your mind will open to new possibilities.

Some people, when they start on the pilgrim's path towards Santiago de Compostela, carry many things "just in case". After a couple of days of walking twenty-four miles a day, every ounce loaded on to the shoulders can be felt. They realise that they can trust in the path and will receive what they need when the need appears. Then they begin to get rid of batteries, torches, alarm clocks, toiletries, etc., to lighten their rucksacks. On a mental level, the first days of walking the path can be full of unnecessary thoughts about what they left behind on leaving home and what is left to go on the path. Little by little, they learn as they go along to walk and enjoy the moment. Their perception sharpens; on being present they see the butterflies, flowers, sky, the countryside, the people. They are able to live in the moment without needing to have their minds taken up with "wanting to get there faster". The mind opens up and, in the pleasure and opening, a renewing inspiration and creativity appear.

Let's look at another example of living well in the moment, doing less and achieving better results. Guests had arrived at her home and Mary had prepared coffee for them. But they wanted tea and herbal teas. So she quickly put the kettle on, going to check whether it had boiled every few seconds, switching it off prematurely and having to put it back on again. Through the anxiety of wanting to make the water boil as fast as possible, she made the process longer. If she had left the kettle on and not interfered, it would have boiled quicker. This is a simple example of what we often do: in our minds we want things to happen faster, and try to make it so, thinking too much, doing more and achieving less, or what we want to happen takes longer and we don't enjoy the moment.

Doing less doesn't mean not doing. It is about being capable of reversing the tendency that we have to think too much, to strive anxiously and get tired before even starting a task. You want to relax, but don't know how to let go of self-imposed pressure to attend to the thousands of details you think you should have done yesterday. Then, when you try to slow down, you feel guilty or disempowered, you think that you have let yourself down.

The objective lies in getting the action to take place without forced effort, doing things out of enjoyment, not obligation. To balance doing with ease and enjoyment at work. Enjoying what we do and keeping the mind happy allows us to work well without stress. To achieve this, we need to live connected to what moves us and provides us with life and vitality, giving us passion and motivating us. Often, anxiety and tensions suck vitality from us and exhaust us, which leads to doing more and achieving less.

To make peace with time, trust is fundamental. (See the chapter: Trust.) There are people who find it difficult to stay with the uncertainty of not knowing and not having answers. They want everything to be clear, under control and planned. They find it hard to be here and now. To live in peace with time we need to be present in each moment, to let go of the previous moment, not hang on to prior events and be available to the new that is seeking to be born.

The joy of working

> We separate joy from work. Our working day is not a day of happiness. We need a festive holiday because – how miserable we are – we don't know how to find festivity at work.
> Rabindranath Tagore[99]

When you work happily, you stay open, with the mental space to be intuitive. Every day brings you new perspectives. You are more creative in your projects and feel the joy of doing your work. To achieve this it is important that your mind is your best friend and your thoughts support you, giving you vitality. A large part of your lived reality depends on your attitude.

It is important to experience and develop your talent at work, understanding what makes you whole. When people feel undervalued and unable to express their talent, they get frustrated because they don't grow. Their inner potential seeks the opportunity to break through. **We need to create spaces to flourish that allow each person to develop their talents and potential, to follow what excites them.**

Another aspect that robs us of joy is expectations. The boss expects you to perform and you expect the boss to evaluate you positively and raise your salary. Both of you are anchored and stuck in your expectations. It would be better to enjoy the process, instead of waiting for the result. If you focus on the process, you concentrate better and are more effective. So the results are better and you enjoy the path without feeling pressured. You are happier, and so is your boss.

We feel pressure from many sides. At work, we feel the pressure to comply with a timetable and deadlines. In relationships, we feel the pressure to meet and fulfil the expectations of others. When we believe that something "bad" or negative can occur if we don't meet the objective or goal we have set ourselves, or that has been set for us, we feel pressured. Fear of failure makes us feel pressure.

Sometimes we pressure ourselves, believing that a bit of pressure helps to achieve what we want; it provides us with adrenalin and energy. It is different when you know you have to do something and have been putting it off until, one way or another, you have to do it. You have little time left, so you finally concentrate, putting all your energy into getting it done, and it gets done. In the long-term, though, repeatedly pressurising ourselves like this leaves us exhausted.

Working under pressure reduces our abilities to think clearly, be discerning and act correctly. Believing that the cause of feeling pressured and stressed are situations, the expectations of others or external deadlines, means there is little you can do to change the habit and sensation of always being under pressure. Nevertheless, people, situations, times change, everything changes, and if we don't strengthen ourselves inwardly, there will always be a reason to feel pressured and live in a stressful manner. If you are under pressure from the outside and also pressure yourself from within, that is a stress timebomb.

It is about learning not to allow the outside to exercise pressure on you on the inside. You can turn the external pressure into an inner vital impulse. You can aim to reach the objective with anxiety, stress and a feeling of suffocation and hurry, or you can reach it with confidence, determination, commitment, perseverance and concentration, staying calm and emotionally stable. How you live it depends on you, on how you position yourself from within, the attitude you choose to have and how you relate to the other.

To alleviate pressure, ask yourself why you feel pressured. Observe the feeling. Where does it come from? What are you afraid of? Don't allow fear to invade you and make you feel stress, anxiety and panicked.

Stopping to observe yourself will help to put a brake on the feeling that you are creating. Look at the thoughts behind the feeling of pressure you experience. "Perhaps I won't arrive on time", "If I don't hand it in on time, I will lose the job", "If I don't do this, they will stop appreciating me." With this kind of thought, the fear is of losing something if you can't meet certain expectations. This fear exercises a pressure that reduces your ability to achieve your objectives. In the process you lose joy and work in fear and anxiety.

For this not to happen, you can change your attitude and the direction of your thoughts. Have thoughts that are trusting and enthusiastic rather than laden with insecurity and fears. To do this, become aware of the beliefs influencing you in the creation of your thoughts. There are thoughts that are determined by your beliefs about success and failure, winning and losing. There are beliefs that are not true, despite the fact that we believe them; they act like a veil preventing us from seeing clearly, generating fearful thoughts and feelings of pressure.

It requires energy to stop and observe, to reinterpret and re-evaluate, to control thoughts and feelings, and to change beliefs. We won't find this energy on the outside; instead it is to be found in the authenticity we carry within. The power of authenticity of our vital core provides us with the energy we need to change. The truth of the healthy core goes deeper than beliefs. Many beliefs are in fact false, causing us anxiety and suffering when we let them influence our perception of reality.

Let's see some examples of how to break the habit of creating pressure and how to tune in to our personal power.

Deadline pressure

The *belief* that causes pressure is that something bad will occur if the work isn't done on time.

The *truth* that relieves the pressure is that nobody loses anything if on occasion they don't manage to hand the work in on time; they might even be honest with the client or whoever is involved, explaining the situation and asking to extend the deadline. Health is the most important thing. If we lose our health because of work pressure, it is more difficult to get it back. Some people lose it completely and end up having serious, sometimes life-threatening, health issues.

Performance pressure

The *belief* that causes pressure is that I might fall short of the performance level I have set myself; maybe I won't reach the bar I have set for myself.

The *truth* that relieves the pressure is that I can only do my best, depending on my capacity at this moment. If I don't reach the bar I have set for myself this time, I will get stronger and learn through this attempt so I can improve next time.

Pressure of the future

The *belief* that causes pressure is that things are definitely going to get worse next week, next month, next year.

The *truth* that relieves the pressure is that everything always changes. There are always reasons for the changes that take place; whether this is worse or better depends on the perspective. We could say that in truth it doesn't get worse, it is simply different.

Pressure of others' expectations

The *belief* that causes pressure is that I have to meet others' expectations; if not, I will lose their approval and this will affect my self-esteem.

The *truth* that relieves the pressure is that I don't "have to" meet anybody's expectations, although I can choose to do so, and that I don't depend on others' approval for my self-esteem. As I commented in the chapter: The value of the self, every encounter with someone could remind us of something we feel inadequate about. We need to respect ourselves and not take others' expectations of us so seriously.

Pressure due to aims and ambitions

The *belief* that causes pressure is that I have to achieve my goals to be happy and successful.

The *truth* that relieves the pressure is that I can be happy without needing to achieve my goals, and it only makes sense to pursue any goal when I am happy; when happy I achieve it more easily.

All feelings of pressure share the *belief* that you might lose something if... The *truth* that relieves the pressure in each case is that you don't have anything to lose, since, in reality, nothing is yours and everything is already in you. In this relief, joy bubbles up, you are relieved of living under the pressures created by the stories your mind invents.

Another question concerns how to feel happiness in adversity. Is it possible to enjoy yourself in adverse conditions? To what extent are we resilient, able to sustain our happiness when problems arise? How do we keep inner power and being without fear, finding happiness even when dealing with adversity? To achieve this we need a high level of compassion and detachment, that is, not to identify with what is happening, involving ourselves without sinking into the quicksand. Allowing life to transpire without having to control it all, not intervening and trying to change what isn't yours to change, makes it easier to be happy. Rachel always used to get irritated by the things that weren't going well at work but was unable to change them. She realised she brought about more change if she let things happen and held on to her good, open and happy attitude. We seem to find it hard "not to do anything and let things be", but sometimes that is what works best and has the greatest impact.

Spaces to care for oneself and be creative

To take care of yourself, you might need your own physical space, one that allows you to be with yourself and stop, reflect, perceive, feel, write, draw, read, create and meditate. Having this space makes it easier to become aware of what you need and how you are on a mental, emotional, spiritual and bodily level; that is, what you are thinking about, what you feel, and how you are in general. Sometimes we inhabit spaces where there are always people, things are always happening, there is noise and movement, and that can make it difficult to stop and listen to yourself. When I have resorted to stopping, in a personal space, it has been very useful, allowing me to realise that perhaps I was very tired and in need of a true rest, or interesting ideas have come to me that I have been able to write down, or the inspiration to paint. We all have creative potential that sometimes doesn't flourish due to a lack of space.

Traditionally, men have tended to have a workspace both at home and outside of it. In contrast, many women don't have their own space at home, and sometimes not outside the home. A personal space makes it easier for us to be with ourselves, allowing us to listen within and create, where our lives are not constantly invaded by children, tasks, situations and other people. It is about finding a space that allows for bodily, mental, emotional, physical, spiritual and creative care.

Sometimes you can feel blocked; you know that something has to emerge from within and express itself, but you don't know what. Perhaps your creative inner potential won't emerge until you take the step of protecting your own space. The moment you take the step, you begin to become clearer and flourish.

Caring for ourselves and others also expresses itself in how we treat the spaces we inhabit. When we go to someone's house and they are not at their best, we can contribute by helping them to tidy and clean. Perhaps we don't know how to, or can't, help them in other aspects, but we can help by caring for their space. It can be liberating for the other person, because at times they are too attached to their things and it's hard to let go of them, or they are so overwhelmed by their situations that they have not taken care of the space they are living and working in. They fill their house with "stuff" and unnecessary objects which take up room and get covered with dust. It is harder to find clarity in a messy place. Creating a clean, tidy, loving and appreciative space makes it easier to care for ourselves and the other.

Feeling comfortable at home makes it easier for us to let go of inner tensions and relax. We can look after ourselves and each other, generating comfort by taking care of details, such as how we prepare and serve food, the lighting we use, how we make an encounter at home special, with candles, decoration, flowers and scents, amongst other aspects. By taking care of the small details we can break the routine and make each moment special.

Being in the world

Our way of seeing the world influences how we feel, our state of mind and what we need. Some perceive the outside world as an unbearable pressure that destroys the vital and creative impulse. They feel traumatised and shut themselves off into a depressing solitude. I like to see the world as a space of great beauty, with multiple possibilities; a place full of life and beautiful people; an abundant natural world full of colours; an earth whose diversity offers many alternatives and great wealth. This vision awakens an attitude in me that is open to being astonished, amazed and enriched; open to learning, sharing and loving. I do not ignore the darker aspects, but neither do I focus on them.

I act resolutely and responsibly to contribute to transforming, reducing or eliminating certain challenging aspects of the world, such as global warming, water scarcity or social injustice. For example, the electricity I consume at home and in my workspace comes from renewable sources. I consume ecological and local products.

Seeing evil, lies and violence causes me worry, but I hold on to what is life-giving and tune in to compassion. There are people who see and feel the world to be a danger, with a constant possibility of deception, robbery and death, a threat to their lives. This causes them fear. They live with fear in their body. In contrast, if they were to see it as a source of beauty that they can enjoy, a place where uncertainty might awaken their desires to live the new, they would experience it as an adventure full of beautiful moments. Otherwise, they will experience it as a tragedy, full of griefs and failures. Depending on how we position ourselves in relation to the world and ourselves, we will live with enjoyment or suffering, trust or fear. There are life stories that are very hard and it is possible that, alone, one does not know or cannot change their position in the face of what they have experienced and are going through. **I believe it fundamental to help each other in being able to lighten our inner burdens and position ourselves in the world, tuning in to what gives us life, breaking our connection with what burdens us inwardly and outwardly.**

A positive attitude, precaution and not taking things personally protect me. It is wise to follow Miguel Ruiz's advice: *"Don't take anything personally.* It is better not to depend on others' opinions, regardless of whether they are good or bad. We all have different visions (agreements) of the world; we don't know whether the other person perhaps had a bad day. All the good or bad that someone may generate, they are, in the first place, doing to themselves."[100]

It's true that there are dangerous places, with an abundance of thieves, rapists and aggressors. Being cautious helps you protect yourself. But if you live fearfully even in your own home, you lose strength and position yourself as a victim in the world. Do you want to keep doing that?

It is important to be conscious of how you position yourself in the world. You can position yourself as defenceless and without strength, or arrogant, thinking you are able to deal with anything. The ideal positioning is neither one extreme nor the other. Imagine that everything is a great play, a piece of theatre, and position yourself according to the scene you are in. Feel yourself to be an actor, dressed for the place and the moment, while knowing that the clothes are not really who you are and that the moment will pass. You can play and laugh, trivialise and know that nothing is permanent, that the happiness of the moment will dissolve and so will the suffering.

You can be alert and peaceful within while watching, not letting yourself be absorbed by what is happening around you. Thich Nhat Hanh is an example, in how he positioned himself in the face of violence and persecution. He carried out many marches for peace in Vietnam, his country of birth. Later, during the war, he argued for peace with the North American soldiers who were killing his people. His attitude was conciliatory and assertive from a position of non-violence. It was an example of compassion in practice.

Another inspiring example of positioning before the world in the face of adversity is the Jesuit Franz Jalics. There was a military dictatorship in Argentina during the time he lived there. He wanted to bear witness to the fact that, despite the very real misery, it was possible to do something for the poor through peaceful means. He went to live in the shantytowns. Many people interpreted this as supporting the guerrillas, and someone from his own community denounced him as a terrorist guerrilla. It wasn't just anyone who denounced him, it was someone from his own community, which must have added to his pain. In May 1976, soldiers detained him and a companion from the mission. In sum, they were hooded, handcuffed and held captive for five months, blindfolded, their hands bound and one leg tied to a heavy cannon ball. They were told they would be released quickly because they were found to be innocuous. However, their hopes vanished as the weeks passed and they were still captives. Franz went through cycles of rage against the people who had falsely denounced them, then impotence, immense sadness, fear and depression. He managed to cry in a huge outburst. Despite these emotional cycles, he continued to meditate and to repeat the name of Jesus. When they freed him, he realised that the months of kidnapping, prison and the proximity of death, together with the constant repetition of the name of Jesus as a mantra, had brought about a deep purification within him. Jalics explains, when narrating this episode of his life, that "Stillness can cause much to move inside a person. On paying attention to Jesus Christ, we communicate with His healing power."[101]

Others position themselves before the world with fears created by their imagination and the phobias in their own minds. That is, something very different to Jalics' experiences. For example, a coaching client of mine was afraid of ending up in prison. Every time he saw the police, James was afraid they would pick him up and there would be a public scandal that would come out in the media. Yet he leads a life of great prudence, of respect towards others, and current rules and regulations. There is nothing in his history that might cause him to end up in a cell. He's a good father, husband, teacher and manager. Nevertheless, his mind creates fictitious realities about being put away in prison, based on films, the news and his own mental inventions. This makes him live fearfully and obsessed.

Sometimes we suffer more from our imaginations than from what is really happening. You create a mental reality and live in your environment out of that mental creation, not perceiving the moment as it is in all its dimensions and perspectives. If you did perceive it, you would realise that on most occasions the threats only exist in your own mind. But even when they do really exist, as in the case of Jalics and his period of captivity, we can devote time to quietening our mind and invoking the healing power of Jesus Christ.

You may live overwhelmed by so many stimuli that your attention is constantly distracted. When you are dominated by circumstances, allowing them to rule your life and emotions, you can feel anger because things are not how you want them to be; sadness because things seem to be getting out of hand and you are losing control over them; upset and disappointment because you put effort and persistence into things, and yet they continue to be the same or worse; fear and worry, because you could be hurt and might sink and drown. When anger, sadness, disappointment and fear invade you, life becomes difficult and you walk on rocky, arid or thorny ground, stumbling into quicksand or stagnant swamps. Perhaps then is the time to learn to surf.

To surf over the waves is to position oneself intelligently in the face of both the unforeseen and the foreseen. We don't know exactly what wave will move forward nor when, but what we do know is that one wave will come, and then another. You deal with one situation and then another, different, one appears. Surfing over the waves of life means to play and create, accepting that the wave is and it is coming, not to judge or fight it. To know how to let oneself fall and swim, take risks, surrender to the other, dance with the sea and movement of the waves, laugh at the game and laugh at yourself. To be flexible and train for the game, playing it.

Caring for yourself is like surfing too. It is to play, create and accept, not judge or fight against, to laugh, fall over and get up. It is to swim and dive, search in the depths, discover beauty and marvel, be flooded with silences and absorbed by an out-of-time dimension where life goes by slowly, not because it passes you by, but because you savour each second. **Let's not forget how important it is to laugh and know how to laugh at oneself. Don't take yourself so seriously.**

There are people who choose solitude and isolation as a way of life. They live in the world by isolating themselves in the mountains or in a small clan, which creates its own world apart from society. They tire of so many winds, currents and waves, and retreat to find tranquillity. They may take their inner and subconscious currents with them and will have to deal with them. They will need a good dosage of meditation to clean those currents, but they will also need to serve in action. If they remain alone, they will end up getting stuck. When we act with the purpose of serving, of being of help, our inner egocentric currents dissolve. In any case, it is possible that the person must return to their family. Jack Kornfield explains many experiences, including his own, of people who have left their family to go to Tibet or to a monastery in another part of the world. In the end, they had to return to their country of origin to resolve and attend to "mundane" matters (inheritances, properties and houses, regaining relationships, taking care of sick people in the family, etc.). The title of his book, *After the Ecstasy, the Laundry,*[102] makes the image clear: after achieving ecstasy in your meditations and monastic life, you have to return in order to wash the clothes that are still dirty.

However, there is a solitude in which one is not inwardly alone because one is connected and in relationship, as Peter Schellenbaum explains: "The true solitary renounces clinging to people, habits of mind and feeling, ideologies and religions, or seeking a foothold wherever it may be. He is so inwardly and intimately linked with the world that it can no longer offer him any foothold or support since he is identical with union with the world, with the world as relationship, with the 'universally flowing subject'. Mark you, he doesn't inflate his subjectivity as far as the world extends. His subjectivity instead melts in the insight that identity, as Buber says, is in between, in relationship. It is splendid to be solitary if the one in whom I am alone (all-one) is the world."[103]

Some choose to live on the high seas; others live moored in port. They neither take risks nor move. Those who are afraid and insist on examining all possible dangers stay in the port. I have family members who avoided sport because any sport presents risks for health and life. You can fracture your bones or have avalanche accidents, or other unforeseen events.

In truth, our choice of attitude in the face of life and the world is very personal. You can choose to live by trusting, launching yourself into the sea. When tired, you can go back to port to recover and care for yourself, not to stay moored there but rather to go out again with full strength to live the adventure of living, cultivating trust as a way of being and relating to each other in the world.

What steps can we take to look after our world? Some questions, some facts...

Do you want to be part of the problem or the solution?

"If we have a common space with limited resources, and everyone thinks only of his own desires, the resources will soon be eradicated. When no one cares for the whole, it means the ultimate deterioration of individual welfare."[104]

Mahatma Gandhi suggested that when making a decision we should ask ourselves if it will also benefit the poorest. His words were: "bring to mind the face of the poorest or weakest person you have ever seen, and ask yourself if the step you are thinking of taking will be of any use to them."[105] For Gandhi, the touchstone of any proposed action was to see how it would affect the most vulnerable person. Therefore, it was not an ideological or general question, but rather human and particular. At the moment, the rich are ever richer and the poor ever poorer. If we were to follow Gandhi's advice, our actions would have greater impact and we would contribute to reducing that difference. For example, buying local, ecological products means you buy a more nutritious product for yourself; contribute to the ecosystem and food sovereignty, and you don't support the farming exploitation of the large food chains that exploit the farmers, make them poorer and impoverish the land with insecticides and transgenic seeds.[106]

Do you embrace the earth with each step you take when you walk? Or do you walk heavily, not conscious of the earth holding you up, causing it to tremble at your passing? Do you take care of what sustains you?

Do you take care of our world with every decision you make? Are you aware of your impact, immediately around you, and in a wider radius, on our world?

You can begin with small things. Taking care of what you already have is important too. Treating each object with affection and attention is to take care of it. So is taking care of what you eat (see about the environmental impact of food on pages 38-39).

When you accelerate the car to go faster, even when a few minutes makes no difference to you, do you think about how you are adding to pollution?

When you buy bananas from far away countries because they cost slightly less than the bananas from your own country or a nearer one, do you know that you are supporting exploitation? What's more, those bananas that have travelled thousands of miles in planes and boats leave a bigger carbon footprint. You are contributing to global warming.

Are you the customer of electricity companies that use fossil fuels or do you use electricity from sustainable sources? Where do you invest your money? Who does your money serve? Taking care of the planet and ourselves also means making sure that the money we earn is used or invested in non-violent ends, that it respects nature and doesn't widen the gap between north/south, poor/rich. For example, we shouldn't invest in projects, investment funds or banks that uphold environmental destruction, the increase in global warming or the arms trade and fossil fuels. Many industries that are toxic for the planet survive due to our consumption. If we didn't consume their products and weren't shareholders, those industries would have to reinvent themselves or die. Being a responsible consumer means being aware of the impact you make with what you buy, why you buy it and who you buy it from. The issue of what we buy is about respecting the world and the environment.

I want to end this part about caring for the Whole with a message from Mother Teresa of Calcutta. If you were to leave the planet for a few moments and observe it from space as someone who nurtures and cares, what feelings arise in you? What do you feel, what inspires you to share?

In the 1990s, Mother Teresa of Calcutta was invited to give the closing speech to "The Architecture of Change" conference in San Francisco, California. The conference brought together all the great management gurus, leaders and senior managers of large organisations and multinationals. Her message was clear, simple and blunt. It was the most highly valued one of the entire conference. She said:

> Do you want there to be change?
> Do you want your people to change?
> Do you know your people?
> Do you love your people?
> If you don't know your people deeply, there will be no understanding between you, and if there is no understanding, there will be no trust.
> Do you love your people?
> Is there love in what you do?
> If there is no love in you, there won't be power or strength in

your people, and if there is no strength, there is no passion. Without strength or passion, nobody will take any risks and, without risks, nothing will change.

7. Compassion and Contemplation

I end the book by asking two questions that are fundamental to the joy of caring for ourselves and each other. One is the need for compassion so that we can transform difficulties into possibilities; the other is the need for a contemplative approach in our daily lives, so we can enjoy caring for ourselves and each other, and do so in a more whole way. Let's look at both questions below.

Compassion

We need to generate a culture of compassion, not only as an ethical duty, but so that trust is cultivated as a way of being and relating to each other in the world.
Pablo d'Ors[107]

Seeing the problems and suffering that inundate us, I have come to the conclusion that to take care of ourselves, our relationships and the planet, it is fundamental to live out of compassion.

Compassion arises from deep love and from understanding the other. We may not comprehend them, nor do we need to, from our rational logical mind; rather, our comprehension comes from the presence encompassing the other in all their dimensions. In compassion, the other's suffering is not contagious, nor do you feel pity. When you allow yourself to be invaded by the other's suffering, it is difficult to help them.

With compassion you uphold the intention and ability to mitigate suffering and alleviate pain. To do this, watch and listen carefully. A deep communication can come into being, that is, one that is real, where you communicate with your body, your look, your feeling and mind. The other person feels better in your communicative presence. Be careful with your thoughts, words and actions.

A word can bring comfort and confidence, it can offer clarity when making a decision, and help someone avoid getting into conflict. The right word at the right moment opens the door to liberation. The person who hears it is given relief.

An action can save someone's life. It can help someone take a decisive step in their career or personal life. An action can be like an embrace for the other person.

An appropriate thought leads to the right words and actions. When you live out of compassion, your presence, your thoughts, words, and actions are transformative.

Compassion is like a healing medicine. It heals the heart from a desert of loneliness and affliction. It heals the mind of negative thoughts overwhelmed by anger, sadness and fear. It heals past traumas by taking on suffering, softening it so it can be released. It heals relationships between individuals, between communities and peoples, reconciling them through forgiveness, comprehension and dialogue.

Compassion is a component of the four immeasurable elements of authentic love, which are comprised of love, compassion, joy and equanimity. Buddhists consider these to be antidotes to negative mental states such as greed, anger or fear. For Thich Nhat Hanh, "they are immeasurable because if you practise them, they will grow in you every day until you come to contain the whole world. You will be happier and the people around you will be too."[108]

Compassion is the virtue uniting the great religions. For Hindus, *Ahimsa* is complete non-violence, the renunciation of what causes harm and the use of violence. It is respect for life. Mahatma Gandhi renewed the ideal and use of *ahimsa* in terms of non-violence by applying it to all areas of life, including politics. In terms of how you live, *Ahimsa* means not being violent towards other living beings, so it means being vegetarian. Compassion for animals is expressed by contributing to their lives, not their slaughter. On a relational level, it means treating the other as you would like to be treated, not doing to others what you don't like to be done to you; this is the golden rule found in all the great religions, one that supposes empathy and compassion.

Compassion is one of the founding stones and basic aims of Buddhist doctrine. It is a form of active love. *Karuna* normally translates as compassion. Compassion includes the *com* – from "accompanying another" or "accompanied by" – and *passion* – understood here as "suffering". But in *karuna* we are not meant to suffer because the other suffers. We *are* supposed to have empathy and be by their side. "We must be aware of suffering, but at the same time keep clarity, serenity and strength so that we might transform the situation. If *karuna* is present, the sea of tears cannot drown us. That is why the Buddha is able to smile."[109]

In Islam, compassion is regarded as one of the cardinal virtues. Of the hundred and fourteen chapters of the Qur'an, all (with one exception) begin with the words: "In the name of God, the Merciful, the Compassionate." Of God's ninety-nine names, the most commonly used are those of Merciful and Compassionate. All Muslims are obliged to feel compassion (*rahmah*) for prisoners, widows and orphans.

In Christianity, compassion is one of the keys to the Gospel and the Christian life. The message of divine compassion runs throughout the Old Testament. The God of the Old Testament is "lenient and compassionate, patient, and merciful" (Psalms 145:8; 86:15; 103:8; 116:5).[110]

Compassion generates reconciliation, understanding and peace. Not only do the great religions preach it but, from the Greeks to our time, philosophers have debated the need and meaning of compassion as an important pathway for coexistence between peoples and relational health. For some, compassion is an emotion, for others a way of reasoning; for some it is contextual, for others universal; some consider it secular, others religious; it can be viewed as a weakness or a personal strength; it is considered an exchange or offering, a gift. Whatever the viewpoint, compassion has been and continues to be a key aspect of our coexistence in the world.

In the *Apology*, Plato contrasts emotions arising from compassion to behaviour governed by reason and justice, arguing that the judge's compassion may prevent him from reaching the right and proper decision.

Aristotle considers that witnessing the undeserved suffering of others affects us, because it might have been us.

For the Stoics, feeling compassion was incompatible with self-rule, or *autarchy*, and peace of mind (*ataraxia*). They regarded compassion as a weakness and disease of the soul. The stoic ideal was to achieve an absence of emotion when facing one's own destiny or that of others. However, they valued the importance of philanthropy and being willing to help others out of benevolence.

According to Augustine, God inscribed the golden rule in the human heart. To have mercy is to accompany the less fortunate from the heart.

St Thomas Aquinas stated that God is not a bureaucrat who applies laws established by a higher authority. As sovereign Lord, God acts out of His being, which is love. Mercy does not cancel out justice but transcends it. Mercy is the fulfilment of justice.

For Rousseau, compassion makes it possible for us to maintain social relationships with others.

Kant offers a more rational perspective. He believes that compassion is not an emotion, but that there are rational reasons driving the ethical behaviour of rational beings. In his *The Metaphysics of Morals*, he states that humans have an indirect obligation to cultivate compassion, as the thought to act out of duty alone is not enough to inspire an active sharing in the destiny of others.

Hegel believed that compassion transcends mere emotion and implies a recognition of the dignity of those who suffer.

Schopenhauer was influenced by the Buddhist belief whereby the barrier between the self and the *you* is dissolved, so that one can find that of self in the other.

Some 20th-century philosophers, such as Martin Buber, offer a perspective based on relationship and dialogue. Humans are made for dialogue, not monologue, living in and through relationships. Compassion is relational.

For Walter Schultz, compassion is the only force against cruelty, which depersonalises and degrades people by turning them into objects of destructive desire. Compassion saves the person from the nakedness of existence when faced with the denial of existence.

Emmanuel Levinas speaks of our obligation to respond to the petitions of others. His concerns lie with the relationship between love and justice.

For Paul Ricoeur, love is unconditional solidarity, the affirmation of the other.

Michel Foucault criticises the logic behind the processes of economic exchange that are based on an abstract notion of justice and power structures.

Jacques Derrida raises the question: how can a perfect and just God forgive rapists without this visiting violence on the victims (who may not agree with God's acts of mercy and forgiveness)?

Jean-Luc Marion writes about the phenomenology of the gift: reality is not something we build; rather, it is given to us. The gift is the sign that one gives of oneself. We give of ourselves and continue to be ourselves.

We have been reflecting and debating on the three major topics of justice, economics and compassion since ancient times. "Economics is the relationship between human beings, their work and the planet Earth that gives us all sustenance."[111]

Egocentric economics and leadership ignore the primary place of compassion and mercy in human nature.

Balancing justice, economics and compassion is not always easy. If we look on a personal level, we might experience family situations where, if guided by what we consider fair, we get stuck in a rigid, angry position arguing for what we consider right. If we choose to be guided by compassion, we will be more sympathetic to each other, and deal better with the situation emotionally. The ideal thing is to be guided by compassionate justice and just compassion, and to place value on caring for one another. If you destroy relationships and become emotionally exhausted by arguing for what you think is just, what price do you pay? If you incorporate compassion when asking for what you think is fair, you will be more open to the other's perception and position and, in that openness, dialogue will be possible. Dialogue is difficult, sometimes even impossible, when there is anger.

Compassion is an innate impulse in a person when they are connected to their positive core, along with love and understanding. People feel fulfilled when they give themselves to the other, accompanying, helping and inspiring them; it makes them feel their life is useful and has meaning. Compassion opens us to the other, and in this opening we connect to and feel each other. This does not mean that you suffer what the other suffers. You don't need to suffer to reduce or eliminate someone else's suffering. Don't make someone else's problem into your own. **Receive the suffering in order to free it.** Don't seek to put the other right or spare them all suffering. As I explained previously, when you want to avoid a butterfly's suffering on leaving the cocoon and open the cocoon to make it easier for it, the butterfly does not break through the cocoon with its own strength, its wings weaken and it dies. It has to open and get through the cocoon itself to become strong and able to fly. If we let it fight to come out alone, it will live. We all have to pass through and out of our cocoons to strengthen ourselves in the transition to the new.

It's not easy because we are always looking for pleasure. We accept and seek pleasure and beautiful experiences. We have an ingrained mechanism in us making us reject and escape from ugly and painful experiences. We try to avoid hatred, dislike, anger and greed. These emotions are compulsive; when they invade us, they trap our minds and hearts, locking us in a prison of suffering that increases exponentially. If they are in you, it is not about avoiding or fleeing from them, but directing compassion towards yourself, for your compassionate being to turn its gaze to your resentful and angry being. Practise *voice dialogue*. Root yourself in your healthy core (see the chapter: The vital core), connect with being compassion, and from your being, enter into dialogue, embracing and receiving your other resentful dimension.

In addition to this dialogue of inner voices, you can meditate and, rooted in your healthy core, in your compassionate being, let the experience be what it is. Be able to see emotion clearly, allow yourself to feel it, and not analyse it or feel bad about feeling it. There's no need to keep going over it. It's about trusting what you're feeling and seeing how you come out of that negative feeling on your own when you don't keep going over it or feeding it in your thoughts. As I explained on page 45, meditation can help a great deal to achieve this. With the practice of meditation you develop a state of inner stillness that allows you to observe what you feel without upsetting yourself with judgment, to apply compassion and equanimity, to be able to find peace in the midst of the storm.

Contemplation

To care is to receive what is and what there is, to welcome it. Don't reject or run from what is. It's about trusting that what is there can be there, and what is can be. In the face of adversity, perhaps we can do nothing except wait for it to dissolve, or perhaps it will be necessary to go through it. Faced with adversity and an adversary, you can be broken, feel resentment, and start bemoaning what is happening to you. Another option is to go through adversity, allowing it to become an opportunity for growth. You take the blows without breaking, growing in your ability to be reborn and give blessings.

To desire, live and appreciate a receptive and welcoming attitude, I need to develop a certain kind of contemplative perspective. To have time, not to be in a hurry. To be able to look at nature in peace. Not to always have urgent things to do and not to obsess over ideas and objectives that I have set myself. To relax and be able to live steadily, without great emotional tensions. This makes it easier to be more sensitive to the people around me.

In contemplation I put myself in a receptive attitude. I open up to receive. I quieten my mind in order to listen. To put myself in a contemplative stance in the company of another person is to open myself to what they might want to share, to listen to and welcome them. However, it is not easy to maintain that attitude. What happens to me is that I am overcome by great enthusiasm to help; almost without realising, I start to offer support by giving advice. If I see a clear solution, based on my experience, I begin to offer suggestions. But when the person in front of me isn't asking for advice, it's better to stay quiet. Or maybe ask a question that opens up their perspective and makes a generative conversation possible. I am learning that I don't have to try to save others from all suffering. "Out of contemplation a more selfless love is born that is content to accompany us."[112]

A contemplative attitude allows me to remain open to reality as it presents itself. I perceive it without letting concepts interfere. Our concepts limit reality. When we stop and silence everything we say about reality and let it speak to us, we are present to the experience of greatness; we look at it and see it.

We realise that the heartbeat of life begins to show itself to us and in us, reality alive in itself. When we silence our mind map that is made of words and symbols, we can transcend and allow the experience of wonder and openness to manifest.

To access this experience, invite it in, take a step beyond yourself. Silence your need to label, manage and understand, go beyond yourself to pay full attention to what is here. What is here is here, inside me, and outside here, in my surroundings. Then I see myself, not out of my own set of needs; I can see the wonder that is here right now in any of us. In this state I enjoy the fullness and mystery of what each of us is.

On the path to silence we say that there is an inside and an outside because we place a boundary between ourselves and the world. On silencing our words, that boundary is weakened and the experience is of unity, non-duality. I experience the world and myself as one. There aren't two. Said in the words of belief and non-belief, religious and poetic, there is no two, everything is one. Therefore, there is no longer any inside or outside; it is all here, in every moment, in each instant, in every element, in everything. You must cross the wall of words, and, in the pure silence, you will see that there is no inside and outside.[113] That greatness is the same in one place and another. Allow yourself to walk towards the greatness and you will be one with the whole and the whole will be one with you. In that unity is bliss, the joy of living.

> Living and being here,
> being here and living.
> Are you here?
> Fully present?
> Feeling the miracle of being here, alive.
> Perceiving the beauty of what surrounds you.
> Opening yourself to the mystery revealed to the eyes of those
>   that look, and

revealed to the heart.
The heart opens itself,
cares and accepts being cared for,
And in that care is true love,
the reason for being and existing.

Notes

1. Pablo d'Ors. "El fundamento de la confianza" [The Basis of Trust]. *ABC*, 24th July 2015.
2. Carl R. Rogers. *On Becoming a Person*. Boston: Houghton Mifflin Company, 1961.
3. Peter Schellenbaum. *The Wound of the Unloved: Releasing the Life Energy*. Dorset: Element Books, 1990 [1988].
4. F. Torralba, L. Sandrin and N. Calduch. *Cuidarse a sí mismo. Para ayudar sin quemarse* [Caring for Oneself: To Help Without Getting Burnt Out]. Madrid: PPC Editorial, 2007.
5. Marianne Williamson, quoted at Nelson Mandela's inaugural speech.
6. Sören Kierkegaard. *The Sickness Unto Death*. Princeton, NJ: Princeton University Press, 1941.
7. Carl R. Rogers. *On Becoming a Person*. Boston: Houghton Mifflin Company, 1961.
8. Francisco Jalics. *Aprendiendo a compartir la fe* [Learning to Share the Faith]. Buenos Aires: Editorial San Pablo, 2008.
9. Carl R. Rogers. *On Becoming a Person*. Boston: Houghton Mifflin Company, 1961.
10. *Ibid.*
11. Francisco Jalics. *Aprendiendo a compartir la fe* [Learning to Share the Faith]. Buenos Aires: Editorial San Pablo, 2008.
12. Miguel Ruiz. *The Four Agreements: A Practical Guide to Personal Freedom*. Toltec Wisdom Collection, 1997.
13. David Bohm. *On Dialogue*. London and New York: Routledge, 1996.
14. Michel Foucault. *The Hermeneutics of the Subject*. Palgrave MacMillan, 2001 [1981-82].
15. *Ibid.*
16. *Ibid.*
17. *Ibid.*

18. *Ibid.*
19. *Ibid.*
20. Edwin Arthur Burtt. *The Teachings of the Compassionate Buddha*. New York: Mentor Books, 1955.
21. Aristotle. *On the Soul*.
22. Tomás Calvo Martínez. Introduction to *On the Soul*, Aristotle.
23. Kenneth J. Gergen. *Relational Being: Beyond Self and Community*. Oxford University Press, 2009.
24. *Ibid.*
25. *Ibid.*
26. Carl R. Rogers. *On Becoming a Person*. Boston: Houghton Mifflin Company, 1961.
27. Kenneth J. Gergen. *Relational Being: Beyond Self and Community*. Oxford University Press, 2009.
28. Sergio Sinay. *Esta noche no, querida: El fin de la guerra de sexos y la aceptación de los valores masculinos* [Not Tonight Darling. The End of the War of the Sexes and the Acceptance of Male Values]. Barcelona, 2004.
29. Friedrich Nietzsche. *Thus Spoke Zarathustra* in Peter Schellenbaum, *The Wound of the Unloved: Releasing the Life Energy*. Dorset: Element Books, 1990 [1988].
30. Franz Jalics. *Ejercicios de contemplación* [Exercises for Contemplation]. Salamanca: Sígueme, 1998 [2013].
31. Rabindranath Tagore. *Sadhana: The Realisation of Life*.
32. Emrah Cüzel, cited by Ulrich Schnabel, *OCIO: La felicidad de no hacer nada* [The happiness of doing nothing]. Barcelona: Plataforma Editorial, 2011.
33. Sergio Sinay. *Esta noche no, querida: El fin de la guerra de sexos y la aceptación de los valores masculinos* [Not Tonight Darling. The End of the War of the Sexes and the Acceptance of Male Values]. Barcelona, 2004.
34. *Ibid.*
35. This paragraph summarises Foucault's explanation in *The*

Hermeneutics of the Subject.

36. Michel Foucault. *The Hermeneutics of the Subject.* Palgrave MacMillan, 2001 [1981-82].
37. David Bohm. *On Dialogue.* London and New York: Routledge, 1996.
38. Ezekiel 11:19. New International Version.
39. As explained by Mark Epstein in *Psychotherapy Without the Self. A Buddhist Perspective.* Yale University Press, 2007.
40. Peter Schellenbaum. *The Wound of the Unloved: Releasing the Life Energy.* Dorset: Element Books, 1990 [1988].
41. Miriam Subirana and David Cooperrider. *Indagación Apreciativa. Un enfoque innovador para la transformación personal y de las organizaciones* [Appreciative Inquiry: A New Approach to Personal and Organisational Transformation]. Barcelona: Kairós, 2013.
42. Norman Cousins. *Anatomy of an Illness as Perceived by the Patient.* New York: Norton, 1979.
43. David Cooperrider. "Positive Image, Positive Action". In: *Appreciative Inquiry: An Emerging Direction for Organization Development,* David L. Cooperrider et al. Champaign, Illinois: Stipes Publishing L.L.C., 2001.
44. Carl R. Rogers. *On Becoming a Person.* Boston: Houghton Mifflin Company, 1961.
45. Karen Kissel Wegela. *What Really Helps.* Boston: Shambhala, 2011.
46. Carl R. Rogers. *On Becoming a Person.* Boston: Houghton Mifflin Company, 1961.
47. Ludwig Wittgenstein. *Tractatus Logico-Philosophicus.* 5.6, 1922.
48. Carl R. Rogers. *On Becoming a Person.* Boston: Houghton Mifflin Company, 1961.
49. W.H. Murray. *The Scottish Himalaya Expedition.* 1951.
50. Simon L. Dolan, Salvador García, Miriam Díez. *Autoestima, estrés y trabajo* [Self-esteem, Stress and Work]. Madrid:

McGraw-Hill, 2005.

51. Pablo d'Ors. "El fundamento de la confianza" [The Basis of Trust]. *ABC*, 24th July 2015.

52. Extract from Ima Sanchís' interview of Ram Prakash. *La contra, La Vanguardia*, 13th September 2011.

53. Miriam Subirana, David Cooperrider. *Appreciative Inquiry*, *Op. cit.*

54. Rabindranath Tagore. *Sadhana: The Realisation of Life*.

55. Peter Schellenbaum. *The Wound of the Unloved: Releasing the Life Energy*. Dorset: Element Books, 1990 [1988].

56. *Ibid.*

57. Anthony Strano. *Explorando los cuatro movimientos* [Exploring the Four Movements]. Barcelona: AEMBK, 2009.

58. Franz Jalics. *Ejercicios de contemplación* [Exercises for Contemplation]. Salamanca: Sígueme, 1998 [2013].

59. William Arthur Ward (1921-1994).

60. Kenneth J. Gergen. *Towards Transformation in Social Knowledge*. London: Sage, 1994.

61. Kenneth J. Gergen and Mary Gergen. *Social Construction: Entering the Dialogue*. Chagrin Falls, Ohio: Taos Institute Publications, 2004.

62. Peter Schellenbaum. *The Wound of the Unloved: Releasing the Life Energy*. Dorset: Element Books, 1990 [1988].

63. Sergio Sinay. *Esta noche no, querida: El fin de la guerra de sexos y la aceptación de los valores masculinos* [Not Tonight Darling. The End of the War of the Sexes and the Acceptance of Male Values]. Barcelona, 2004.

64. Marguerite Duras (1914-1996).

65. Carl R. Rogers. *On Becoming a Person*. Boston: Houghton Mifflin Company, 1961.

66. Francisco Jalics. *Aprendiendo a compartir la fe* [Learning to Share the Faith]. Buenos Aires: Editorial San Pablo, 2008.

67. Carl R. Rogers. *A Way of Being*. Boston: Houghton Mifflin Company, 1980.

68. Carl R. Rogers. *On Becoming a Person*. Boston: Houghton Mifflin Company, 1961.

69. Deepak Chopra. "Intimidad [Intimacy]". In: VV.AA. *El arte de vivir*. Barcelona: Editorial Kairós, 2015.

70. Francisco Jalics. *Aprendiendo a compartir la fe* [Learning to Share the Faith]. Buenos Aires: Editorial San Pablo, 2008.

71. Sergio Sinay. *Esta noche no, querida: El fin de la guerra de sexos y la aceptación de los valores masculinos* [Not Tonight Darling. The End of the War of the Sexes and the Acceptance of Male Values]. Barcelona, 2004.

72. *Ibid.*

73. *Ibid.*

74. Fritz Perls. *Sueños y existencia* [Dreams and Existence]. Buenos Aires: Cuatro Vientos, 1990.

75. Carl R. Rogers. *On Becoming a Person*. Boston: Houghton Mifflin Company, 1961.

76. Carl R. Rogers. *A Way of Being*. Boston: Houghton Mifflin Company, 1980.

77. Martin Buber. *I and Thou*, 1923, as quoted by Carl R. Rogers.

78. Carl R. Rogers. *A Way of Being*. Boston: Houghton Mifflin Company, 1980.

79. Otto Scharmer. *Addressing the Blind Spot of Our Time: Leading from the Future as It Emerges*. Cambridge, Massachusetts: Society for Organizational Learning, 2007.

80. Franz Jalics. *Ejercicios de contemplación* [Exercises for Contemplation]. Salamanca: Sígueme, 1998 [2013].

81. Carl R. Rogers. *A Way of Being*. Boston: Houghton Mifflin Company, 1980.

82. Miguel Ruiz. *The Four Agreements: A Practical Guide to Personal Freedom*. Toltec Wisdom Collection, 1997.

83. Sergio Sinay. *Esta noche no, querida: El fin de la guerra de sexos y la aceptación de los valores masculinos* [Not Tonight Darling. The End of the War of the Sexes and the Acceptance of Male Values]. Barcelona, 2004.

84. Franz Jalics. *Ejercicios de contemplación* [Exercises for Contemplation]. Salamanca: Sígueme, 1998 [2013].

85. Thich Nhat Hanh. *Teachings on Love*. Parallax Press, 2007.

86. Rabindranath Tagore. *Sadhana: The Realisation of Life*.

87. *Ibid.*

88. Francisco Jalics. *Aprendiendo a compartir la fe* [Learning to Share the Faith]. Buenos Aires: Editorial San Pablo, 2008.

89. Rabindranath Tagore. *Sadhana: The Realisation of Life*.

90. Eckhart Tolle. *A New Earth: Awakening to Your Life's Purpose*. London: Penguin, 2005.

91. David Cooperrider et al. *Appreciative Inquiry: An Emerging Direction for Organization Development*. Champaign, Illinois: Stipes Publishing L.L.C., 2001.

92. Sonja Lyubomirsky. *The How of Happiness*. UK: Sphere, 2007.

93. Carl R. Rogers. *A Way of Being*. Boston: Houghton Mifflin Company, 1980.

94. *Ibid.*

95. Carl R. Rogers. *On Becoming a Person*. Boston: Houghton Mifflin Company, 1961.

96. Thich Nhat Hanh. *Teachings on Love*. Parallax Press, 2007.

97. Francisco Jalics. *Aprendiendo a compartir la fe* [Learning to Share the Faith]. Buenos Aires: Editorial San Pablo, 2008.

98. Peter Schellenbaum. *The Wound of the Unloved: Releasing the Life Energy*. Dorset: Element Books, 1990 [1988].

99. Rabindranath Tagore. *Sadhana: The Realisation of Life*.

100. Miguel Ruiz. *The Four Agreements: A Practical Guide to Personal Freedom*. Toltec Wisdom Collection, 1997.

101. Franz Jalics. *Ejercicios de contemplación* [Exercises for Contemplation]. Salamanca: Sígueme, 1998 [2013].

102. Jack Kornfield. *After the Ecstasy, the Laundry*. London: Rider, 2000.

103. Peter Schellenbaum. *The Wound of the Unloved: Releasing the Life Energy*. Dorset: Element Books, 1990 [1988].

104. Kenneth Gergen. *Relational Being: Beyond Self and Community*.

Oxford University Press, 2009.

105. Alan Axelrod. *Gandhi, CEO*. New York: Sterling, 2010.

106. See Wikipedia on *Food sovereignty*.

107. Pablo d'Ors. "El fundamento de la confianza" [The Basis of Trust]. *ABC*, 24th July 2015.

108. Thich Nhat Hanh. *Op. cit.*

109. *Ibid.*

110. Walter Kasper. *El de la misericordia* [Mercy]. Santander: Sal Terrae, 2012.

111. Joan A. Melé. *Dinero y conciencia, ¿a quién sirve mi dinero?* [Who Does My Money Serve?]. Barcelona: Plataforma, 2009.

112. Francisco Jalics. *Aprendiendo a compartir la fe* [Learning to Share the Faith]. Buenos Aires: Editorial San Pablo, 2008.

113. Miriam Subirana. *La gran liberación: Heartfulness y Mindfulness* [The Great Liberation. Heartfulness and Mindfulness]. Barcelona: Kairós, 2015.

SPIRITUALITY

O is a symbol of the world, of oneness and unity; this eye represents knowledge and insight. We publish titles on general spirituality and living a spiritual life. We aim to inform and help you on your own journey in this life.
If you have enjoyed this book, why not tell other readers by posting a review on your preferred book site?

Recent bestsellers from O-Books are:

Heart of Tantric Sex
Diana Richardson
Revealing Eastern secrets of deep love and intimacy to Western couples.
Paperback: 978-1-90381-637-0 ebook: 978-1-84694-637-0

Crystal Prescriptions
The A-Z guide to over 1,200 symptoms and their healing crystals
Judy Hall
The first in the popular series of eight books, this handy little guide is packed as tight as a pill-bottle with crystal remedies for ailments.
Paperback: 978-1-90504-740-6 ebook: 978-1-84694-629-5

Take Me To Truth
Undoing the Ego
Nouk Sanchez, Tomas Vieira
The best-selling step-by-step book on shedding the Ego, using the teachings of *A Course In Miracles*.
Paperback: 978-1-84694-050-7 ebook: 978-1-84694-654-7

The 7 Myths about Love...Actually!
The Journey from your HEAD to the HEART of your SOUL
Mike George
Smashes all the myths about LOVE.
Paperback: 978-1-84694-288-4 ebook: 978-1-84694-682-0

The Holy Spirit's Interpretation of the New Testament
A Course in Understanding and Acceptance
Regina Dawn Akers
Following on from the strength of *A Course In Miracles*, NTI
teaches us how to experience the love and oneness of God.
Paperback: 978-1-84694-085-9 ebook: 978-1-78099-083-5

The Message of A Course In Miracles
A translation of the Text in plain language
Elizabeth A. Cronkhite
A translation of *A Course in Miracles* into plain, everyday
language for anyone seeking inner peace. The companion
volume, *Practicing A Course In Miracles*, offers practical lessons
and mentoring.
Paperback: 978-1-84694-319-5 ebook: 978-1-84694-642-4

Your Simple Path
Find Happiness in every step
Ian Tucker
A guide to helping us reconnect with what is really important in
our lives.
Paperback: 978-1-78279-349-6 ebook: 978-1-78279-348-9

365 Days of Wisdom
Daily Messages To Inspire You Through The Year
Dadi Janki
Daily messages which cool the mind, warm the heart and guide
you along your journey.
Paperback: 978-1-84694-863-3 ebook: 978-1-84694-864-0

Body of Wisdom
Women's Spiritual Power and How it Serves
Hilary Hart
Bringing together the dreams and experiences of women across
the world with today's most visionary spiritual teachers.
Paperback: 978-1-78099-696-7 ebook: 978-1-78099-695-0

Dying to Be Free
From Enforced Secrecy to Near Death to True Transformation
Hannah Robinson
After an unexpected accident and near-death experience, Hannah
Robinson found herself radically transforming her life, while a
remarkable new insight altered her relationship with her father, a
practising Catholic priest.
Paperback: 978-1-78535-254-6 ebook: 978-1-78535-255-3

The Ecology of the Soul
A Manual of Peace, Power and Personal Growth for Real People
in the Real World
Aidan Walker
Balance your own inner Ecology of the Soul to regain your
natural state of peace, power and wellbeing.
Paperback: 978-1-78279-850-7 ebook: 978-1-78279-849-1

Not I, Not other than I
The Life and Teachings of Russel Williams
Steve Taylor, Russel Williams
The miraculous life and inspiring teachings of one of the World's
greatest living Sages.
Paperback: 978-1-78279-729-6 ebook: 978-1-78279-728-9

On the Other Side of Love
A woman's unconventional journey towards wisdom
Muriel Maufroy
When life has lost all meaning, what do you do?
Paperback: 978-1-78535-281-2 ebook: 978-1-78535-282-9

Practicing A Course In Miracles
A translation of the Workbook in plain language, with mentor's notes
Elizabeth A. Cronkhite
The practical second and third volumes of The Plain-Language
A Course In Miracles.
Paperback: 978-1-84694-403-1 ebook: 978-1-78099-072-9

Quantum Bliss
The Quantum Mechanics of Happiness, Abundance, and Health
George S. Mentz
Quantum Bliss is the breakthrough summary of success and
spirituality secrets that customers have been waiting for.
Paperback: 978-1-78535-203-4 ebook: 978-1-78535-204-1

The Upside Down Mountain
Mags MacKean
A must-read for anyone weary of chasing success and happiness
– one woman's inspirational journey swapping the uphill slog for
the downhill slope.
Paperback: 978-1-78535-171-6 ebook: 978-1-78535-172-3

Your Personal Tuning Fork
The Endocrine System
Deborah Bates
Discover your body's health secret, the endocrine system, and
'twang' your way to sustainable health!
Paperback: 978-1-84694-503-8 ebook: 978-1-78099-697-4

Readers of ebooks can buy or view any of these bestsellers by clicking on the live link in the title. Most titles are published in paperback and as an ebook. Paperbacks are available in traditional bookshops. Both print and ebook formats are available online.

Find more titles and sign up to our readers' newsletter at http://www.johnhuntpublishing.com/mind-body-spirit

Follow us on Facebook at https://www.facebook.com/OBooks/ and Twitter at https://twitter.com/obooks